ROMANISM AND THE GOSPEL

ROMANISM
AND THE GOSPEL

BY

C. ANDERSON SCOTT,

D.D. Cantab., Hon. D.D. Aber.
Westminster College, Cambridge

AUTHOR OF "CHRISTIANITY ACCORDING TO ST. PAUL"
"NEW TESTAMENT ETHICS" "EVANGELICAL DOCTRINE—BIBLE TRUTH"

CHURCH OF SCOTLAND
COMMITTEE ON PUBLICATIONS

121 GEORGE STREET, EDINBURGH
232 ST. VINCENT STREET, GLASGOW

1937

Printed in Great Britain

CONTENTS

CONTENTS

INTRODUCTORY NOTE

THE debate with Rome is a perennial one. Going down to the foundations of our faith and worship, and involving the whole conception held of the Christian religion, it is inevitably renewed in every generation, and in these pages its significance is set forth with singular freshness and power for the instruction of our time. The writer wields a practised pen; his learning is unimpeachable; and as readers of his earlier *Evangelical Doctrine—Bible Truth* are aware, he has made this field his own. It is a privilege to be permitted to introduce so valuable a work to the public. The enquirer will find in it sure-footed guidance. I commend its persuasive teaching to all who prize the freedom and spirituality of the Gospel, and who are concerned for its defence against an historic perversion which is ever changing yet still remains the same.

ALEX. MARTIN.

EDINBURGH,
January, 1937.

INTRODUCTION

ST. IGNATIUS the martyr Bishop of Antioch (A.D. 110) has a fine saying, "Where Jesus Christ is, there is the Catholic Church." It is the first recorded use of the word "Catholic," and as Ignatius used it, it meant "Universal." And when he wrote, the Church *was* universal, though it was not uniform. From Jerusalem to Rome, in Palestine, Asia Minor, Greece and Italy, communities of Christians known as "churches" knew themselves as members of a universal Fellowship, the Catholic Church. They were bound together by a common faith, expressed on its intellectual side in the Apostles' Creed and manifested on its moral and emotional side in a deep devotion to Christ, and in a moral ideal which, while it incorporated what was permanent in the ethical system of the Jews and what was valuable in the best thought of the Greeks, far "exceeded the righteousness" of the Pharisees and of the philosophers, by the common consciousness of a relation to God in Christ. It was the unity, or spiritual Oneness for which Jesus prayed that it might be manifested by His followers. And its effect was seen, as He had foretold, in the rapid spread of the new religion, even as the effect of individual devotion to Christ was seen in its most impressive form in the heroic endurance of persecution, the unflinching acceptance of martyrdom by thousands of His followers.

I

It was this common consciousness, not any external union which came to expression in Ignatius' word *katholiké*. The scattered Christian communities kept touch with one another by means of letters, visits and the sending of assistance when needed. There was no central control. The local churches were guided at the first in accordance with Jewish practice, by boards of "presbyters" or older men, who were also known as "bishops" or overseers. Only two steps were needed to bring about what we know as the episcopal system. The first was that one of the board of elders became permanent chairman; the second that his authority was extended to include several congregations and ultimately many congregations in a wide area, his "diocese." These steps were taken at different times in different parts of the Church, so that there was a time when its organisation was far from uniform. Already before the time of Ignatius (A.D. 100-110) there was probably in some parts one who was called "*the* bishop," responsible for a number of congregations. This system of "monarchical bishops" spread rapidly, but the bishops themselves were only loosely held together, many of them in active correspondence with one another, groups of them meeting from time to time for consultation, but none claiming jurisdiction over others. A further step towards centralisation combined a number of dioceses into a Province, over which was set a dignitary who was known from the fifth century onward as "the Patriarch." Four or five of these Patriarchates stood out from the rest in consequence of the distinction which attached to their sees. And these entered upon a struggle for supremacy which lasted for centuries, a struggle amongst themselves, and a united struggle against the Bishop of Rome, although he was never known as a Patriarch. With the final victory of the Pope the organisation of the Roman Catholic Church, as we know it, was complete, and its character determined. It was to be a Fascist State, a dictatorship.

This claim to supremacy over all the other Bishops, which was made on behalf of the Pope, appealed for support to our Lord's commission to Peter. It made itself heard in various quarters from the beginning of the fifth century onwards, and in spite of repeated protests from those who resented any such domination met with an ever-widening acceptance. It was furthered by the transfer of the Imperial capital from Rome to Constantinople, which left the great city without an Emperor. To a large extent the Pope came to supply his place. Still more propitious to the Papal claim was the fact that the Catholic Church itself broke in two. The final breach took place in A.D. 1054, but for two centuries before that there had been strife between the East and the West. The causes were originally personal and political. The Pope excommunicated the Patriarch of Constantinople; the Patriarch excommunicated the Pope. He charged the Church of the West with unorthodoxy, because of one word which it had added to the definition of the Holy Spirit in the Nicene Creed. It is interesting to note that he further charged it with using unleavened bread at the Eucharist, and with insisting on a celibate

3

priesthood. The Eastern Church calls itself the Greek Orthodox Church, but it is none the less representative of the ancient Catholic Church of the first seven centuries. If it was "Catholic," then it has done nothing since to forfeit the title. And so we must, on this ground alone, deny to the Roman Church its claim to be recognised as *the* Catholic Church. There is a Greek Catholic Church and a Roman Catholic Church.

A second crisis in the history of the Roman Church took place in the sixteenth century, when the Church in Western Europe was again divided in consequence of what is known as the Reformation, and ever since then the Reformed Churches and the un-Reformed Church have confronted one another as rival interpretations of Christianity. The difference, or rather the differences, between them go so deep that it would be foolish to entertain any hope of reconciliation. On the other hand, the differences in doctrine, worship and organisation which distinguish the Reformed Churches from one another do not go nearly so deep; and in so far as these Churches may be truly described as "evangelical" they are conscious of a true spiritual unity, which finds many opportunities of expression and cultivation. For this reason it is quite legitimate to speak of the Reformation as issuing in a separation between the "Reformed Church" and the Church which is un-Reformed.

The need for Reformation in the Church began much earlier than is commonly understood. It began, indeed,

as early as the second century after Christ, and it continued with increasing force and ever-widening scope
until the sixteenth century brought the reformation at
least of a large part of the Church in the West. And
this Reformation itself was far from being the first
attempt to bring about reform, for which in all probability great numbers of Christians were at all times
thirsting and calling. On the contrary, it was the last
of a long series of efforts for reform in doctrine, or in
administration, or in ethical standards. All these
efforts began within the Church. They were all "Protestant" in the sense that they all represented a protest
against the falling away of the official Church from the
Gospel deposited in the New Testament, or against
crying abuses of ecclesiastical authority. Many of these
movements were promptly branded as "heresy," not
because they could be shown to be contrary to revealed
truth, but because they represented rebellion against
established authority. They were stamped out by
force, though some of them persisted for centuries as
"sectarian" Churches. Montanists, Donatists, Pauli-
cians, Albigenses, Cathari, these are only the best
known of the communities of "Catholic" Christians
who gathered together at the trumpet-call of some
leader who denounced either the message of the Church
as defective, perverted, or, in some cases, false, or the
morality which it tolerated as sub-Christian. All of
these movements proved abortive, and died away,
until we come to the Reformation, and that was successful, though only partially so.

The beginning of the need becomes evident when we

compare the Christian literature of the second century with that of the first, the Epistle of Clement to the Corinthians with the Gospel of John (the two were practically contemporary), the letters of Ignatius with the letters of St. Paul, or again the work of the Apologists with the Synoptic Gospels. The result is, indeed, startling. To state conclusions, the reasons for which must be given subsequently, the Church had taken over from Judaism principles which were in contradiction to the teaching of Jesus. It now found the teaching of St. Paul either unintelligible or unpalatable. It was indifferent to the historical Jesus as He is depicted in the Gospels, indifferent to nearly everything therein recorded which belongs to the fact that He "was found in fashion as a man." If (as was the case) the leaders of Christian thought at this time and for long afterwards concentrated on Christ as a Divine Being, the Word "made flesh," now Risen and Glorified, it thought of His work for men mainly if not exclusively as the bringing of Knowledge, the acceptance of which secured immortality to men. We must not forget that we whose habit it is to begin with the Jesus of the Gospels, are confronted by the opposite danger, the danger of stopping short at an uninterpreted death and the bare fact of a resurrection, and so losing sight of the living Lord, whose presence with His people both interprets and transforms life.

The real nature of the situation at the beginning of the second century has for long been obscured by the exaggerated deference shown especially by English scholars to the writings and opinions of the "sub-

Apostolic Fathers" who flourished in that century. It has been commonly assumed that they, standing as they did in direct succession to those who first gave literary shape to the Christian tradition, and bearing testimony in their lives to its vital force, must be taken to be reliable witnesses to its contents, and to have preserved the Gospel in its purity. But we know now that this was not so. Causes which we shall have to examine had been at work, with the result that both in what it asserted and in what it overlooked the Church had already departed seriously from the Gospel. In asserting that salvation was to be obtained by merit, it stood in contradiction to the teaching of Jesus, and in its failure to do justice to the teaching of St. Paul it cut itself off from a true understanding of the Gospel. The need for "reform" in doctrine in the sense of a return to the full revelation in Christ was therefore already present at the beginning of the second century, and the subsequent history of the Church showed a progressive departure from "the truth as it is in Jesus," and also, in spite of many noble exceptions, a progressive departure from the spiritual character and the ethical ideals which had been the marks of its divine origin.

The need for a reformation in doctrine, worship and moral standards can only be appreciated if we approach the study of the "Catholic" Church with the witness of the New Testament clearly before our minds.

THE WITNESS OF THE NEW TESTA-MENT

THE New Testament, containing as it does the record of the life and teaching, the death and resurrection of Jesus Christ, and also the record of men's earliest experiences of the presence and saving power of the living Christ, must be the authoritative standard for Christian thought and conduct. The interpretation of Christ, His person and His Work and its application to the changing conditions of human life is the work of the Holy Spirit; and the instruments which He teaches us to use in arriving at a true interpretation are sound learning, the witness of the educated Christian conscience and the experience of those in the past or the present who can be described as adequately Christian. If we believe, as we do, that the Spirit does guide such "into all truth," we must be prepared to recognise the results of such guidance, whether of individuals or of groups, in the progress and clarification of thought. Thus we do not deny the possibility of what may be called development of doctrine, or growth of organisation; that would be to deny the Holy Spirit. But at the same time we have a duty to ourselves and those who come after us to insist that no "development" can be legitimate which runs counter to principles which clearly enter into the fabric of New Testament revelation. We must assume that the Holy Spirit is con-

sistent with Himself; if there is progress in the interpretation of the mind of God in relation to men, it
must be a forward, not a backward, progress.

We begin then by setting down some of these fundamental principles which are found in the New Testament, whether they appear there for the first time or
not. The following, at least, are certain. (1) The
universality of sin, conceived not only in terms of
sinful acts, but as a state of moral separatedness from
God, the loss of that "image of God," the glorious
goodness of man's first estate. (The question of the
origin of sin is of no practical importance.) In the
parable of the Two Sons Jesus has shown us two types
of this separatedness, in one son who defiantly shook
off the father's control and fellowship, and in the other
who never at any time transgressed his commandment, and yet was hopelessly alienated from him. And
Jesus has given us a list of some of those things (actions
and dispositions) which "defile a man," that is, inevitably lead to this state of separatedness from God
(Mark vii. 20). Paul gives a similar list and declares
that "they which do such things shall not inherit the
kingdom of God" (Gal. v. 21); they are "cut off from
the life of God" (Eph. iv. 18).

(2) The universal and unconditioned Grace of God
available for every man who opens his heart to receive
it, God's love coming forth to meet man in his manifold
need of repentance, reconciliation, peace and power.

(3) Faith, an energy set in motion in the human
spirit in response to the approach of God in "Christ
and him crucified"; faith which expresses itself in love,

and so in itself establishes between a believer and Christ a bond which guarantees growth in holiness. "By grace ye are saved through faith" (Eph. ii. 8).

(4) Reconciliation, the restoration of fellowship between God and man which has been destroyed by sin; something which takes place between the individual man and God, but is mediated or brought about through the sacrificial death of Christ. Of this we have clear foreshadowings in the Gospels. "The Son of man came not to be served, but to serve, and to give his life a ransom for many" (Mark x. 46), meaning "in order to bring about their deliverance." "This cup is the new covenant in my blood" (Luke xxii. 20), meaning, "This represents the new covenant between God and men, which is to be sealed by my sacrificial blood," when "God will forgive their iniquity and remember their sin no more" (Jer. xxxi. 34). Sayings such as these were illuminated for our Lord's disciples by the events which followed them, the Crucifixion and the Resurrection, and by the experience of the power of the living Christ to save which became theirs through faith in Him. In the light of these events and of this experience these sayings were interpreted and emphasised by St. Paul ("God was in Christ reconciling the world unto himself"), by St. Peter ("He died, the just for the unjust, that he might bring us to God").

(5) The guarantee of these things and of yet better things to follow (1 Cor. ii. 9) was found in the gift of the Holy Spirit. Long before there was any doctrine of the Holy Spirit there was among those who had faith

10

in Christ an experience of His presence and His power. His coming to individual men or to groups of men was recognised as a gift direct from God, in accordance with the word of Jesus in Luke xi. 13, "how much more shall your heavenly Father give the Holy Spirit to them that ask him?" St. Paul is equally clear, "God hath sent forth the Spirit of his Son into your hearts" (Gal. iv. 6). It is faith that opens the door to the coming of this all-comprehending gift. Men help each other towards the receiving of it by proclaiming Christ. "Faith cometh by hearing, and hearing by the proclamation of Christ" (Rom. x. 17 R.V.; Gal. iii. 1, 2; Eph. iv. 20, 21). At a later stage men were further helped to realise the coming of the gift through the symbolic act of "laying on of hands" (1 Tim. iv. 14; Heb. vi. 2). And by a natural yet most unfortunate transition the idea sprang up that the receiving of the Spirit was due not to faith, but to this action by other men. The immediate results of what Paul calls "the hearing that leads to faith" (Gal. iii. 2) are a heart "flooded with the love of God" (Rom. v. 5), "newness of life" (Rom. vi. 4) and a joyful recognition of God as Father, of ourselves as "sons," and of other men as brethren. The ultimate result is entering into possession of "every good thing which is ours in Christ" (Phm. 6), "righteousness and peace and joy in the Holy Ghost."

(6) In many other ways the Spirit works in and with the Christian for his growth, morally, spiritually and intellectually. And perhaps the most important of these is the gathering together in one body, one sacred society, of all those who have faith in Christ. The New

Testament has different names for this society, the Fellowship, the Unity, the Body of Christ, the Church. To call it a "voluntary society" is both true and untrue. It is true inasmuch as every man belongs to it by his own consent. It is untrue inasmuch as his consent is a response to a summons or invitation which he receives from Christ or from the Spirit. (In respect of practical experience these two are interchangeable.) That there is a sacred Society for him to join is due to the act of God, in accordance with the purpose of Christ, and the result of the operation of the Spirit.

Up to this point in the life-history of a Christian he has been acting and reacting as an individual—however much he may have been helped by a Christian atmosphere or by Christian witness. It is as an individual that he has been in contact with God, or with God in Christ, or with the Holy Spirit (these are but different ways of stating the same experience). He is never so truly alone as in the act of repentance, in experiencing the divine forgiveness, or in entering into peace with God. In all these experiences he requires no other mediator than the Lord Jesus Christ. But this isolation comes to an end the moment after he has closed with Christ. He rejoices to know himself a member of the household of God, a fellow-citizen with God's people (Eph. ii. 19), one of a sacred Society, the Body of Christ, the Church. This comes about independently of action on the part of any organised body of Christians. Such a body may admit him to be one of its members, and may lay down such conditions of membership as it sees fit. Similarly, it may for its own reasons exclude him from membership, but as a human institution it has neither the power to admit him to the fellowship of Christ, nor the power to exclude him from it.

"Where two or three are gathered together in my name, there I am in the midst of them." That is the charter of the Church according to the New Testament. "Name" means person as known, and to be gathered in His name is to come together with a common consciousness of Christ as Saviour and Lord, in the fellowship which that common consciousness creates. It is a fellowship which includes not only His believing people, but Himself. And in that double unity of man with man and of men with Christ, we have the Church. As Ignatius put it, "Wherever Jesus Christ is, there is the Church."

Of course the Church as thus described cannot continue long to exist, cannot propagate itself from generation to generation unless it forms for itself some kind of organisation; and, as a matter of fact, every body of Christians which claims to be part of the Church of Christ has developed an organisation of its own. No criticism attaches to it on that ground. On the other hand, the same principle of criticism must be applied to its organisation as we have seen to apply in regard to doctrine. If it is to be recognised as truly a Church of Christ, it must be able to show that it does not in any important respect contravene the teaching of Christ.

It will be observed in connection with each of these principles that the Pauline interpretation is an illustration of expansion or development which is legitimate. It offers no contradiction of the mind of Jesus as it is made known to us through the Gospels. It is, indeed, continuous with it, representing a harmony which, however we may account for it, justifies, so far as these fundamental principles are concerned, Paul's claim to have the mind of Christ. If it were possible for us to ask Paul to explain how this came about, he might answer thus: "By the great mercy of God, and through my faith in Christ, I have come into a spiritual relation to Him so close, so intimate (Gal. ii. 20), that I seem to be standing at His side. I see the things which He sees, the great realities, not so clearly, not so perfectly as He sees them; still I see them, and I try to help other men to see them."

The New Testament therefore must remain our standard of Christian Doctrine and conduct. The principles which it reveals to us are such as do not require "the wise and prudent" to understand or expound them. They can be discovered by simple people who seek for them with unprejudiced minds and unresisting wills. And any system of thought and morals which challenges or contradicts these principles must find it hard to justify a claim to be a Christian Church at all. It is in applying the standard of the New Testament that we raise the question whether Dean Inge is or is not justified in his sweeping judgement: "The Church of Rome *as an Institution* is apostate from the Gospel."

14

THE NEED FOR REFORMATION

WE cannot but believe that if anywhere we have "the mind of Christ," it is in the New Testament. We gladly accept the promise that the Holy Spirit will lead the true followers of Christ "into all truth." We recognise that that implies advance or development in the apprehension of "truth as it is in Jesus," deeper penetration into the revelation which is embodied in His teaching, His character, His death and resurrection, and His power to save. But we cannot be persuaded of the validity of any interpretation of, or addition to, the witness of the New Testament which runs counter to basic principles of Divine truth therein made known. Still more unhesitatingly do we reject any developments which represent a return to earlier or lower forms of religion, from which Christ lived and died to set men free.

Now, it is important to recognise that when tested by this criterion, the Church betrays its need, its great need of reformation much earlier than is commonly understood. The need is in fact patent even before the second century, and only went on increasing in the centuries which followed. We have also to recognise that the movement in the sixteenth century to which we give the name of the Reformation was not, as many are apt to think, the first movement of the kind, or that it was due to an unprecedented outburst of hostility against the doctrines and practices of the Roman Church, an unprecedented outbreak for which Martin Luther was responsible. The truth is that it was the last of a long series of such movements directed towards reform. The others had either failed through internal weakness, or been overwhelmed by bloody persecution. This one succeeded, although its success can only be described as partial, whether we have regard to the range of its criticism or to the area over which it won its way in Europe.

This need for reformation, already present at the beginning of the second century, becomes clear only through a careful study of the Christian literature of the period. This is very scanty in the first half of the century, when, as has been said, Christianity "passed through a tunnel." Between the Epistle of Clement (A.D. 96) and the works of Justin Martyr (*circa* 150) we have only the letters of Ignatius, the Epistle of Barnabas, the Didache or Teaching of the Twelve Apostles, and two short letters from Pliny to the Emperor Trajan, enquiring how he as Provincial Governor of Bithynia is to deal with Christians. Some scholars would add the Pastoral Epistles of St. Paul and the Epistle of St. James. For the second half of the century we have the Apologists headed by Justin Martyr, Hermas and Irenaeus, with one or two other writers, together with what has been recovered of the works of Marcion.

The letters of Ignatius stand by themselves. For the rest, even a rapid reading of them, with the New Testament before our minds, raises the question, what has happened? And the question becomes more in-sistent when we recall that the same period was a time not only of rapid extension of the Church, but of severe though sporadic persecution throughout the Empire, of unflinching loyalty to Christ and heroic endurance of indescribable tortures and of martyrdom on the part of hundreds of Christians, and not only of famous ones like Ignatius and Polycarp, Perpetua and Blandina, but of an unnumbered multitude "who did their deed, and scorned to blot it with a name." The problem arises when we compare the documents of the period with the New Testament on the one hand and with the record of suffering for the name of Christ on the other. For the notes of triumphant faith, of sure hope, of unbending courage which ring through the one and are echoed by the other, are not heard in the literature (except in Ignatius).

We may approach a solution of the problem and also discover the beginnings of the need for reformation through a rapid examination of the Epistle of Clement to the Corinthians, written towards the end of the first century.[1] Let us begin by trying to realise what it meant to be a Christian worshipping, say, at Corinth, towards the end of the first century. He lived in a busy and prosperous commercial city not distinguished like Athens for interest in art or literature or philosophy, but notorious all round the Mediterranean for the immorality which flourished there unchecked. He belonged to a community or congregation which

[1] What follows is largely founded on the brilliant studies of Harnack and Lietzmann. Such quotations as are not from the Epistle itself are from one or other of these.

owed its origin to St. Paul. The Apostle had paid at least two visits to the city some fifty years before, on one occasion had remained there some eighteen months, and when he departed left behind him a considerable body of Christians, including the chief ruler of the Synagogue and many others who "hearing believed, and were baptized." To this congregation Paul had sent four letters, two of which are in our hands. We hear of one of them from Clement, who, writing from Rome in A.D. 96, bids the Corinthians "take up the epistle of the blessed Paul the Apostle," and then refers to a passage which is found in the First Epistle. This tells us that a letter of St. Paul was preserved at Corinth at the end of the first century, that the Christians there had access to a copy or copies of it, and that Clement at Rome knew it and probably had a copy. And we may suppose that the letter, being held in honour by the congregation, would be read from time to time at public worship.

The same letter of St. Paul gives us in the fourteenth chapter a picture of worship as it had been conducted in the early days at Corinth. It was so spontaneous and unregulated that the Apostle had to urge that only one person should speak at once, and that all things should be done "decently and in order." And his advice was not given in vain. At Corinth, as elsewhere, the public worship of Christians fell into an order which was modelled on that of the Jewish Synagogue, with the important addition of the observance of the Lord's Supper. The conduct of the service was in the hands of officials known as Elders or Presbyters, and also as

Bishops or Overseers. (The one name would be familiar to those who had been Jews, the other to those who had been Gentiles.) These had been chosen by the congregation. But there was another class of officials, who moved from place to place, and were understood to have been called of God to serve the churches in general, and to have received a special gift of the Holy Spirit to qualify them for their work. Of these the "Apostles" had died out, and the "Prophets," who spoke as they were moved by the Holy Spirit, were dwindling both in numbers and in influence. The resident officials were beginning to take their place and to exercise the authority which at first had belonged to the Apostles and Prophets.

Public worship on the Lord's Day would include, along with prayers and "psalms and hymns and spiritual songs," reading from sacred and authoritative books. What books or rather documents of that character were available for the use of the church at Corinth in A.D. 96? Many would still be apt to say, "The Bible." But that, of course, is a mistake. The Old Testament was available in a collected form, the sacred literature of the Jews. But before the documents which form our New Testament were collected and recognised as authoritative Scripture ("canonised"), fifty years and more had to elapse. The process which led to this end had three stages. Let us put them down, and mark their approximate dates. The first stage is, of course, the writing of the documents. All the genuine letters of St. Paul must, of course, have been written before his death, round about A.D. 63. The

Synoptic Gospels, Matthew, Mark and Luke, were completed between 73 and 85. But we must remember that the material of which they were composed (and a great deal more of the same kind) had been circulating through the churches during the previous forty years (A.D. 32-73). And already as early as A.D. 55 sections which were afterwards incorporated in our Gospels may have been crystallised into written form. The whole narrative of the Passion of our Lord, as we have it in Mark, was probably the first of these. Anyone who was able to tell something which had been said or done by Jesus would be eagerly listened to. The Fourth Gospel appears to belong to the nineties.

But these documents were scattered over many different churches, and the second stage was the collecting of them together. It was not until about A.D. 110 that Paul's Epistles began to circulate as a collection. Clement knew some of them. Ignatius seems to have known most if not all. The collecting of the Gospels followed soon after, and this stage was completed about A.D. 140 by the gathering together of all the documents which form our New Testament.

The third stage was still to follow, the canonisation of all these documents, their recognition as authoritative Scripture. The beginning of this stage can be observed in Justin Martyr (about A.D. 150) and the completion of it in Irenaeus a generation later.

Now, the significance of all this for our purpose is that in the absence of authoritative documents of their own, a body of Christians, like the church at Corinth, had to rely for written teaching and edification upon the Old Testament, and we shall find that this was one of the chief reasons why already in the second century there was urgent need for "reform." Almost inevitably the Church fell away from the full Gospel of Jesus Christ.

That it did not fall further away than it did was due to circumstances which helped to preserve through these fifty years a living tradition, and to the power of the "message about Christ" to change the lives of men.

The situation was unlike any with which we are familiar. The memories of men in those days were long, whereas ours are short. Conversation occupied the place we give to books and newspapers. Life was free from most of the distractions by which we are beset. Concentration to a degree which we hardly know was easy. And those who had found in Christ their Saviour could, after the needs of work and home had been attended to, fix their attention upon Him and all that He meant.

And what He "meant" included not only all that they could learn about His life and teaching, but all that they knew of the teaching of Paul and other Apostles, all that they knew of Christ's power to save manifested in the experience and lives of others, as well as their own experience of the living Christ, realised especially in the Fellowship of the Church and in the breaking of bread at the Lord's Supper. These Christians were "alive in Christ," but they were "babes in Christ" when it came to giving an orderly account of the principles of the Gospel. And part of the account which they did give was wrong. Ideas

21

which were more akin to Judaism than to the Gospel of Christ filtered into the minds of those who had only the Old Testament to depend upon as a written authority, and it is of such filtration that we find evidence in the literature of the period.

The Epistle of Clement arose out of a dispute which had taken place at Corinth. The non-resident officials, Apostles and Prophets, had died out or lost their prestige. Inevitably, some of their functions passed to the resident officials, Presbyter-Bishops and Deacons. These had been elected by the congregation. Was their office one to be held for life, like that of the Apostles, or was it held for a term of years or at the will of the people? News of this dispute came to the ears of Clement, one of the Bishops at Rome, and he wrote this long and important letter, in which he brings every argument he can think of to support those who asserted the permanence of the episcopal office. What gives his letter great importance is that he writes on behalf of the Church at Rome, and his attitude to the Gospel may be taken to be the same as that of his fellow-Christians there.

The first thing we notice in this letter is the extra-ordinary disproportion in the number of allusions to, and quotations from, the Old and the New Testaments. Of these, Clement has about a hundred and twenty from the Old Testament against only a dozen passages which show a knowledge of the New. The scantiness of these references is all the more remarkable in a writer who in his argument relies very largely upon illustrations and quotations from recognised authority.

In search of these he has ransacked the Jewish Scriptures. Indeed, nearly every important person mentioned there (together with a good many unimportant ones) is brought in to enforce the plea that he is making. "Large portions of this Epistle might have been written in a Synagogue at Rome " (*Harnack*).

On the other hand, his allusions to what we know as contained in the New Testament are very few. He congratulates the Corinthians that they pay attention to the words of Christ, "having carefully stored them in their hearts." But of these he quotes only two, and as one of them is altered he quotes probably from memory and not from the written Gospels. He makes no reference to the active ministry of Jesus, to the miracles or the parables, or to His Crucifixion (except in so far as he several times refers to the "blood"). And though he repeatedly refers to the living Christ, he has only two references to the fact of the Resurrection. Once only does he refer to St. Paul by name. But we must not be misled by the famous saying, "Take up the Epistle of the blessed Paul," followed by an adaptation of a verse in First Corinthians. It is rather an expression of conventional respect than evidence that he was familiar with the Epistles, or that he understood and accepted the teaching of the Apostle. All that was specifically characteristic in Paul's exposition of Christianity he systematically ignores. "Sin," "faith" in the sense which Paul gives to the word, and "reconciliation" fall into the background. Isaiah liii. 1-12 is quoted in full, but is used to illustrate the fact that Christ was humble-minded, with no suggestion that it

c   23

throws light upon the significance of His death. Clement has indeed curiously few references to sin. Most of these occur in quotations from the Old Testament, and in only one is any connection suggested between Christ and the forgiveness of sin. Similarly, the doctrine of the Holy Spirit has lost all its vitalising force. Clement claims that he has written "through the Holy Spirit," refers to "the Spirit of grace poured out upon us," but in the half-dozen other passages in which he mentions the Spirit it is always as the inspiration of the Old Testament; "the Holy Spirit saith." It is hard to resist the conclusion that either Clement did not know the Pauline Gospel as "a Divine Force unto salvation," or that he had rejected it. We may keep open the possibility that he rejected it because he did not understand it. That possibility is definitely suggested in 2 Peter iii. 16.

One essential feature of Paul's teaching Clement definitely rejects, when he says, "We are saved by works and not by words." He adopts the teaching of the Pharisees. "Alms maketh atonement for sins." "Whoso honoureth his father maketh atonement for his sins" (Ecclesias. iii. 3, 30). "Almsgiving saves from death and purges away all sin" (Tobit xii. 9). This doctrine was so strongly held that the word "righteousness" had become a synonym for "alms." "Do not your righteousness before men" (Matt. vi. 1). The falsity and the danger of the doctrine are seen in the complacency with which the Pharisee in the Parable approaches God, with what Paul calls "boasting," or making a proud claim (Rom. iii. 27). "To him that

24

depends on works is the reward reckoned not of grace but of debt" (Rom. iv. 4). He insists on a contractual relation with God, whereas Christ calls him to a filial one (John i. 12; Gal. iii. 26; iv. 7).

But it is not Paul only that Clement and the writers who came after him rejected. It was something central in the teaching of Jesus, and its subsequent rejection by the Catholic Church has changed the character of its religion. The Apostle frequently puts into a proposition what Jesus had put into a picture or a parable. When he says, "By grace ye are saved through faith . . . not of works" (Eph. ii. 8), we are apt to think of it as an idiosyncrasy of the Apostle. But it was only what Paul had somehow caught from Jesus. Let us look at some of the passages which convey this teaching. There is the Parable of the Labourers in the Vineyard (Matt. xx. 1-16). That Parable, so far from teaching that a man is rewarded by God according to his work, teaches the exact opposite, namely, that there is no relation between the amount of work done by man, even when it is done at the command of God, and any benefit which he receives from God. The annoyance displayed by those who had worked all day at the action of their employer shows how difficult it is for us to accept this teaching, how contradictory it was to the theory of the Pharisees. But the Parable means that for the Pharisees to think of merit or desert on the one side as being met by corresponding payment on the other is to misconceive man's relation to God, indeed to misconceive God Himself. What He bestows on man— righteousness, salvation, or whatever else it be—is and can be nothing that man has earned. It is the free and sovereign gift of God.

The same teaching comes out more clearly in the Parable of the Pharisee and the Publican. The Pharisee presents himself before God full of complacency. He has done all that was required of him and more. He had paid tithes not only on the products of his fields but on the products of his garden. He claims, therefore, not only merit, but superfluous merit, what the Catholic Church came afterwards to speak of as "works of supererogation." The Publican makes no claim at all; he simply casts himself on the mercy of God; and it is of him that Jesus says that he returned home right with God rather than the Pharisee. It seems to us very simple and in accordance with our conception of God. That conception is, however, one which has come to us through Christ, and we have to be at pains to realise how completely the inference drawn from it, that salvation is by grace, contradicted the theory of the Pharisees.

There is a third passage (Luke xvii. 7-10) which conveys the same teaching in a different form. Dr. Montefiore describes this as "a highly noble, notable and important passage." It concludes, as we remember, with the words, "So also do you, when you have done all that was commanded you, say, We are unprofitable servants, we have done what it is our duty to do." The clue to the meaning lies in the word "servants" (*douloi*), which describes persons who serve under compulsion. Their time to the last minute of the day, their strength to the last ounce of it, belongs to their master. They

26

can never create a margin beyond what is required of them. In that sense they are "unprofitable." Strangely enough, the same point was made by the Roman moralist, Seneca. He asks, "Can a slave confer a benefit? Is his service not merely a duty to his lord, which as it springs from constraint is not deserving of gratitude?" This passage confirming the other passages makes it abundantly clear that according to the teaching of Jesus a man who thinks that by serving God either from fear or from self-interest he can earn merit in God's sight is abysmally mistaken.

It is not necessary to do more than point out that Paul had seized this truth, or as he would have said, been seized by it, and that he recognised it as all but central to the Gospel of Christ. He describes in a moving way his own prolonged but hopeless attempt to achieve a righteousness of his own. He had put our Lord's teaching to the test. He had abandoned the attempt to obtain a righteousness of his own and had sought and accepted a righteousness that was from God, and he had found that Salvation, past, present and to come, was his.

To forget this fundamental teaching of our Lord and then to deny it would evidently be a very serious departure from Christianity according to Christ. Yet this was done by the sub-apostolic Church. Again there was no one to blame for it. Those on whom blame rests are their successors, who with the New Testament in their hands resisted all attempts to get back to its teaching.

Clement knew the teaching of Paul, partly through

some of his Epistles with which he was acquainted, partly through living tradition. He knew it, but he had not assimilated it. He speaks of Christians as being "justified by works." He shows no grasp of what Paul understood by faith. Faith for him means obedience to the will of God. He has the word "justification," but it is little more than a word to him. His idea of redemption is only a meagre one, and it is difficult to show that he had any serious view of sin. He pleads long and earnestly for obedience to God's will as revealed in the Old Testament, but has little to offer as motive for such obedience.

What has been said of Clement applies equally to others of the sub-apostolic writers. A strange idea that it is the duty of the Christian to be as good as he can, and that any more than that will be counted to his credit, appears in various forms. The strange work of Hermas is quite frank about works of supererogation. "If," he says, "thou doest any good over and above the commandment of God, thou shalt obtain greater glory for thyself." Hermas thus encourages the idea of surplus merit, which even at this early period "completely stifled the understanding of the Gospel" (*Loofs*). The *Teaching of the Twelve Apostles*, which was a handbook of Christian morality and worship, goes yet a step further: "Of whatsoever thou hast gained by thy hands, thou shalt give a ransom for thy sins."

Thirty years after Clement we find in Justin Martyr evidence of the same grave failure to understand Christianity as a religion of redemption from sin by grace. That "Christ Jesus came into the world to save sinners" is the witness of the New Testament. It follows that, as Dr. Inge has said, "to ignore sin is to make Christianity incomprehensible." But for Justin Martyr, and for other writers of the second century, sin and the way in which our Lord has dealt with it seem to have little or no interest. For them the "work of Christ" consists practically in the communication of a knowledge of God which is philosophically correct, together with a system of moral instruction.

That there was a real danger for the Christian Church arising from this subtle influence of Judaism is shown by the anxiety on the subject which was expressed by several of the sub-apostolic writers. The theory of fasting which is criticised by Hermas is definitely that of the Jews or Pharisees. Ignatius takes up more general ground. "If we are still living according to Judaism, we confess that we have not received grace." "It is monstrous to talk of Christianity and practise Judaism." And the Epistle of Barnabas (of uncertain date, between A.D. 80 and 120) is written for the express purpose of warning Christians not to adopt the standards or practices of Judaism. Such warnings might be effective in checking a disposition to revert to external forms of Judaism, and yet fail to check the subtler influences of frequent and uncritical contact with the documents of the earlier faith.

In the spheres of administration and of worship the same influence of Judaism displays itself in language which was pregnant with consequences in the future. Thus when Clement says, "To the High Priest his

29

proper ministrations are allotted, and to the Priests the proper place has been appointed and on Levites their proper duties have been imposed," all he is really doing may be drawing attention to the orderliness of the ministry in the Jewish Temple, but in fact he is laying the foundation for the threefold ministry in the Christian Church, "Bishops, Priests and Deacons." When he adds (using the word for the first time), "The layman is bound by the ordinances for the laity," we see the beginning of the distinction between "clergy" and "laity" as rulers and ruled, which has since been carried to such lengths in the Roman Church, and against which the Reformers strove to set the New Testament conception of "the priesthood of all believers." And when he writes that the Apostles "appointed their first converts to be bishops and deacons of the future believers," he opens the door to the theory of Apostolic Succession.

It would be a mistake to describe all this as a falling back into Judaism. What it means is that the Church had adopted certain principles which were fundamental to Judaism but alien to Christianity. And for that reason the need for reform in the sense of a return to the New Testament conception of Christianity was already present at the end of the first century. The need was not created only by the progressive deterioration in doctrine and practice which manifested itself during the Middle Ages. Neither did the Church have to wait till the sixteenth century for attempts at reform. These also began very early, though their significance is probably veiled for us by the fact that they are

labelled as "heresies" in our Church Histories. Both
Montanism and Marcionism, which sprang up towards
the middle of the second century, no doubt had or
came to have features which the Church was justified in
repudiating. But for all the extravagances into which
they may have been led, they aimed at recovering some
of the features of New Testament Christianity which
had been neglected or repudiated by the orthodox
Church. And it is probably not altogether a coincidence
that both these movements followed soon upon the
collection and circulation of the Epistles of St. Paul
or of the New Testament as a whole. In Montanism
it is not difficult to see an enthusiastic attempt to
recover for the Holy Spirit the place assigned to it in
Pauline congregations, and foretold for it in the Fourth
Gospel, to bring back a prophetic or charismatic
ministry, to give again to women the place they had
occupied in Christian worship (1 Cor. xi. 5), and to
revive the emphasis on the transcendental character of
the Kingdom, which expressed itself in the hope of our
Lord's return, and is the counterpoise to the danger of
worldliness in the Church. In Marcion we see the
discovery of the Pauline interpretation of Christianity
leading to a rejection of the Pharisaic theory of salvation by works, which in the fierceness of its conviction could not stop short of a rejection of the Old
Testament and even of the God by whom the legalistic
system was believed to be inspired. These movements
started by Montanus and by Marcion developed into
organised "Churches" which offered a serious challenge
to the "Catholic" Church. That they maintained their

existence for two or three centuries, in the face of authority and persecution, shows how serious Christians, with the New Testament in their hands, criticised the dominant Church, and felt the need for reform.

There is, however, a second factor in the thought and style of this letter. Clement was not a Jew. He was a product of Hellenic civilisation, and while his style reflects the influence of the accepted models in Greek epistolary literature, the contents of his letter betray the influence of famous teachers of morals in the pagan world. Most of the virtues which he emphasises, and which he calls upon the Corinthians to display, were familiar in the Stoic teaching, in Epictetus or Seneca. In his approach to the situation which confronted him at Corinth we see a greater reliance upon "wisdom" than on "religion." The function of Christ was rather to confirm what Paul calls "the wisdom of men" than to bring the "power of God" to bear upon human character.

But side by side with these factors in Clement's thinking there is another very different one, which is of the greatest significance, one which incidentally points to the solution of the problem with which we started. It may be described as emphasis on the Impact of Christ, emphasis on facts about Christ without any penetrating attempt to relate them to one another, or to bring them together in a system of theology. "There was as yet no Church-theology at all, but only certain fundamental features which were proclaimed, along with these a hundred scattered fragments of a theological kind, and drawn from various sources, in which edification was sought almost without selection" (*Harnack*). According to Clement, Christ is "the Lord," the child or son of God; together with the Holy Spirit He belongs in an exclusive sense to God. "Have we not one God, and one Christ and one Holy Spirit?" The Kingdom of God is also called the Kingdom of Christ. "In Christ Christians have their faith, their instruction, their calling, their salvation, their love, their walk and conversation."

These and other experiences which belong to the Christian are all such as radiate from the living Christ. Less light is thrown on the way in which Christians enter on such experiences, except that Clement lays great emphasis on the "blood" of Christ. "Let us fix our gaze on the Blood of Christ, and let us know that it is precious to his Father, because it was poured out for our salvation, and brought the grace of repentance to all the world." But there is no trace of the explanation suggested by our Lord's words about "a ransom" or "the new Covenant," nor yet of Paul's interpretation of the Cross.

There is, however, evidence in the New Testament to show that at the beginning the Fact of Christ, based on certain great events in history, but as yet unexplored or incompletely explored, formed the core and heart of the Christian Message. Thus Paul declares that when he first came to Corinth he had made up his mind "to know nothing among you save Christ, and him crucified." We put a comma after "Christ" to show that this was the primary subject of his preaching,

33

Christ risen and glorified, living and present with His people (Matt. xxviii. 20), and the proclamation of Christ as crucified, Christ as Saviour, followed, to show the relation of Christ in glory to needy men. Elsewhere Paul emphasises the two parts of this message separately. To the Ephesians he says, "Ye have not so learnt the Christ-message, seeing that, as I take it, ye have heard it, and in him have been taught, as truth is revealed in Jesus." And the Galatians he reminds that Christ has been "placarded before them as one who has been crucified." The spear-point of the message lay in the triumphant witness to Christ as a living Saviour, and what gave weight to the witness was the content of the second clause of the Apostles' Creed, signifying a belief "in Jesus Christ his only Son our Lord," corresponding to the belief "in God the Father Almighty." The clauses which follow summarise the truths concerning Jesus which taken together make up the Fact of Christ. Faith, hope and love sprang from it and gathered round it. Men said, "I know *whom* (not, *what*) I have believed."[1] It is further to be remembered that this consciousness of the Living Christ and of being united to Him by faith which "expresses itself in love" was confirmed and nourished by the weekly celebration of the Lord's Supper, whereat He "was known of them in the breaking of bread." That is to say, He was really present. They felt Him to be so, more vividly than at any other time. And if they

[1] In a private letter, written by Professor Burkitt shortly before his death, he said, "I have come to see that the 'Life of Jesus' contained in the Creed rather than the narrative in the Gospels was from the first the wide-spread Life known to Christians."

heard the words of Jesus recorded in the Fourth Gospel, "I am the Bread of Life," they would understand them, because they found that the Living Lord communicated Himself to them as He had done to the disciples, and so became the nourishment of the Life which is eternal. It was this experience which Ignatius described, giving it a materialising touch, as "the medicine of immortality."

The name of Ignatius may remind us that in that heroic figure we have the palmary example of this concentrated devotion to Christ issuing in the long-drawn-out martyrdom of that interminable journey from Antioch to Rome, with the Colosseum awaiting him at the far end. "From Syria to Rome," he writes, "I am fighting with wild beasts by night and day, bound to ten 'leopards,' that is, a company of soldiers. I long for the beasts that are prepared for me." And what inspires him is the Fact of Christ, attested by the great events. "To me the Charters are Jesus Christ, the inviolable charter is his Cross and death and resurrection, and the faith which is through him."

It is needless to say that this fourth factor in the thinking of Clement is of the highest importance. It explains the utter loyalty to Christ which was displayed by uncounted men and women in many generations, who after leading pure and sacrificial lives sealed their faith by their blood. It further accounts for the saintly characters of men and women who have served Christ in and through the "Catholic" Church. For the "Catholic" Church, like the other Churches of Christendom, has always had those among its members who said, "I am of Christ," and left it at that.

The letter of Clement is genuinely Christian in so far as it sets Christ at the centre of religious experience and makes loyalty to Him the criterion of right conduct. But the genuine Christian life which lies behind it is one born of living witness and guided, so far as it is specifically Christian, by living example. It is Christian life without a theology, that is to say, without an ordered account of the origin of the new life as designed and provided by God, and without a coherent presentation of Jesus as the divine Teacher and example of how that life is to be lived. In the situation of the moment it was almost inevitable that it should be so. But the situation was obviously one of great danger. The Church was beset by influences which threatened to mould its thinking and to change its character in a non-Christian direction. And we must not forget the other factors, the subtle influence of Jewish ideas mediated through the Old Testament, the pervasive influence of an intellectualist atmosphere acting as a chill upon Christian enthusiasm. We recall also the eclipse which had obscured all that was most characteristic in the teaching of Paul. There are, therefore, three factors which are effectively present in the Christianity of Clement, and presumably in the Church at Rome. There is no sign of any tension or contradiction between them; neither is there any fusion of them. And it is easy to see what will happen if the third factor is challenged either by one, still more if by both, of the first two. It did happen, and the result is seen in "Catholicism."

"This letter is a document in three colours: Old Testament religion as understood by later Judaism, the moral idealism of Hellenistic thought, and the fact of Christ's appearance (together with the Message and the new ethical ordinances)—these comprise the content of the letter. This threefold combination constitutes Christianity as it presented itself to Clement and to the Church. What offered itself therein was, however, Catholicism as religion; no essentially new element required to be added" (*Harnack*).

The full results of the influence of pre-Christian ideas on the Church's system of thought did not show themselves until subsequently, but they were very serious; they will come up for fuller consideration later on, but meanwhile may be summarised thus.

(1) The New Testament doctrine of salvation through faith was replaced by the Jewish doctrine of salvation by "works of the law," divine grace by human merit.

(2) The Jewish conception of religion as conditioned by the individual's relation to a community or institution took the place of the Christian conception of a personal relation of the individual to God which led to his incorporation in the Body of Christ, the Church.

(3) The old legalistic idea of the moral demands of God as embodied in a written code came back in full force, and denied the work of the Holy Spirit as one who both "makes alive" and guides men into knowledge of the will of God.

(4) The "spiritual" or immaterial sacrifices which Christians were to offer instead of the material sacrifices of the old dispensation, such as prayer, praise and the surrender of themselves (Rom. xii. 2; 1 Pet. ii. 5), were replaced by a materialised conception of sacrifice in the doctrine of the Mass.

(5) The figure of Jesus the merciful Saviour who came to call sinners to repentance, and whose invitation is, "Come unto Me, all ye who labour and are heavy laden," practically disappears, and its place is taken by the figure of Messiah, a merciless and implacable Judge, whom His Mother tries, and often in vain, to move to pity. This change manifests itself completely about the fifth century, but may be reckoned among the perversions of the Gospel which began quite early to call out for reformation.

The need for reformation therefore which began before the end of the first century was in the first instance a need for reform in doctrine, for the elimination of specifically Jewish principles which had perverted the truth of the Gospel, for the restoration to its due place of the Pauline doctrine of salvation by grace through faith, and for the repudiation of the attempt to commend Christianity to the intellectual world by exhibiting it as itself a philosophy of a higher kind. For such a reformation Christendom had to wait for many centuries. And in the meantime the imperfect or false interpretations of Christian truth bore fruit in corresponding developments in the life, worship and organisation of the Church. Legalism took the place of the freedom of the Spirit. Sacramentalism made the living Word subservient to itself. Step by step an organisation was built up which culminated in the exaltation of the Pope to absolute supremacy and the transformation of the Church into a political institution employing the religious instincts and needs of men to minister to human greed, pride and the lust for power. And alongside of these developments there went on a progressive moral deterioration, culminating in the degradation of the Papacy in the fourteenth century and the arrogance, cruelty and iniquity which made the Church an offence to God and man.

All this is, of course, partially offset by the appearance of men and women whose devotion to Christ, purity of life and noble service throw into relief the shortcomings of the Church, and Societies or Orders of men and of women which for a time at least preserved a high standard of Christian morality and heroic self-sacrifice. But the experience of many of these individuals in their relation to the Church and the history of many of these Societies only illustrate further the fundamental insincerities and inherent worldliness of the system as a whole and of the hierarchy, which, be it remembered, regards itself as " the Church."

The need for reformation went on deepening and widening, in spite of many attempts at reform, all through the Middle Age. When the appointed time came it was not, as we shall see, the doctrinal system of the Church which was, in the first instance, criticised and attacked, but the Church's moral impact upon

Europe. The discovery followed that the un-Christian character of this impact was due to the perversions of the Gospel which the Church had, rather helplessly at first, but culpably afterwards, accepted for its own.

PERVERSIONS OF THE TRUTH AS IT
IS IN JESUS

SUCH, then, was the general situation at the end of the first century. Certain serious perversions of the truth of God as it had been revealed in Jesus had already made their appearance in the teaching of the Church. And these continued to dominate the thinking of poorer thinkers and to confuse the thinking even of the better thinkers for many centuries. Other perversions, such as the worship of Saints and of Mary, the doctrines of the Mass, of Purgatory and of Penance, appeared later. All that can be done here is to examine the Roman Church as it presented itself in the sixteenth century with a fixed, final and "irreformable" system of doctrine, and as it presents itself now to the minds of hosts of its adherents to-day. This distinction calls attention to a very real difficulty which meets us when seeking to make clear the true character of Romanism. There are at least three grades or forms of authority which may be appealed to in support of various doctrines and practices. There are, first, the decisions of various Councils, culminating in those of the Council of Trent (A.D. 1545-1563) and the decisions of Popes for which equal authority is now claimed. Secondly, there are the opinions of individuals, great theologians and Fathers of the Church from Irenaeus to Thomas Aquinas and Liguori. The opinions of such men cannot be set against the decisions of the Councils or of the Pope, but they may qualify them, by introducing novel considerations, and we are left uncertain how far such considerations are to be looked on as valid. And thirdly, there is the great crowd of popular beliefs and practices, many of them closely related to age-long superstitions, which have come down from pagan times, but now form part of the religion of the rank and file. Even when it cannot be said that these are authorised by the Church, yet they are tolerated and often encouraged by the inferior Clergy. And a much heavier weight of responsibility rests upon this Church in the matter than would rest upon any other Church in similar circumstances. For the Roman Church claims and exercises the right to lay down for its adherents what they shall believe and how they shall behave in the minutest particulars. A Church which has suppressed within its own borders movements like Gallicanism and Jansenism, Molinism and Modernism, cannot be excused for tolerating among its members in different parts of the world beliefs and practices which are definitely at issue with the faith once delivered to the Saints. If the complaint is sometimes heard that it is difficult to find out what are the doctrines taught and held in the Reformed Churches, it is even more difficult to discover what is really taught and held by Roman Catholics. Not that there is any want of clearness or firmness in the Decrees, say, of the Council of Trent, but within certain broad outlines there is almost endless variation in their interpretation and application. There is a useful illustration in the attitude of the Roman Church to Divorce. As over against the Reformed Churches it plumes itself on the fact that it is obedient to the express teaching of Jesus, in refusing to countenance divorce for any reason whatever. Nevertheless, what comes to the same thing, marriages can be "annulled" and are "annulled" with the consent and by the authority of the Church. The decision is that the marriage is at an end because it could never be; the parties were related to one another within "the prohibited degrees." And as both godfathers and godmothers are held to be as truly related to their godchildren as their natural relations, the opportunities for finding a flaw in the marriage are multiplied, and so every year many marriages are "annulled." It is in this kind of way and by means of "dispensations" of all sorts that the Church can modify in practice some of its most rigid principles.

A still more extraordinary illustration of the way in which the Roman Church can play fast and loose with fundamental principles of social morality is to be found in the attitude which it has recently adopted to marriage in Italy. "Since the Concordat with Fascism the Church in Italy may and actually does authorise religious marriage, carrying no civil rights, between persons one or other of whom is already married to someone else. This extraordinary procedure is authorised and explained by Government Circulars and the instructions of the Church to its officers."[1]

[1] Giorgio Quartaro, *La Femme et Dieu*, 1930, quoted in *Hibbert Journal*, January 1936.

There is one cause which accounts for some of these perversions, or lends support to them—one for which the Church itself cannot be held responsible. That is that now for many centuries the official or authorised Scriptures have been not the Hebrew and Greek originals, nor yet any translation into any national language, but the Latin Version of the Bible known as the Vulgate, which was made by Jerome towards the end of the fourth century. This gradually displaced older translations into Latin, and ultimately the Council of Trent, anxious "that it should be made known which of all the Latin editions of the sacred books in actual circulation is to be deemed authentic," ordained and declared that "the same old and Vulgate edition which has been approved by the long use of so many ages in the Church itself is to be held for authentic in public readings, discourses and disputes, and that nobody may dare or presume to reject it on any pretence."

Here again, in spite of the authority of the Council of Trent, and the clearness of this declaration, it is difficult to ascertain how far it is observed in practice, and the situation is further complicated by the fact that there are two or three editions of the Vulgate itself which show textual variations from one another. But these considerations do not affect certain consequences which arise from the setting up of Jerome's version as the officially recognised Scriptures of the Church. Some of these consequences are felt through mistranslations, such as in Romans v. 12, "In whom (Adam) all sinned" (for, "inasmuch as all have sinned"), a mistranslation upon which was built the doctrine of original or birth sin. Another illustration is found in the rendering of the word for "repentance" by poenitentia, which suggests instead of a complete change of mind or of attitude to God, self, and the world, sorrow for sin and (when the word appears in English as "penance") a means of escaping the penalty of sin. Scarcely less unfortunate, because much more widely distributed, has been the inevitable result of translating Greek words into Latin ones when the very genius of the language leads to the producing of a different impression. It was often impossible to provide a Latin word to convey the exact sense of a Greek one. So it came about that in many cases Latin words were used to translate Greek ones, because they were conventional and current rather than because they were exact, with the consequence that with the words there came into the passages ideas which had no association with the Greek words. And thus the Vulgate, while making the New Testament available to the Latin-speaking world, is in many cases a distorting medium. Some theology would have been written differently, and some not at all, if the Greek words which are represented by *gratia, justificare, propitiatio, redimere, imputare, praedestinare, poenitentia* had been the current coin of discussion.[1] The serious results of this substitution of the Vulgate for the original Greek of the New Testament are not confined to the Roman Church; for many of these Latin words have passed over into our English versions, and into our own theological

[1] See the important article by the Archbishop of Dublin in *Exp. Ti.*, xlii. 8.

vocabulary. To take one example, how much mis-understanding has been caused by the rendering, "he that doubteth is damned" (Rom. xiv. 23), of words which mean, "he that wavereth (Jas. i. 6), is uncertain whether he is doing right, is self-condemned." Which-ever way he acts, he will think himself wrong. The word "damn" here and in Romans iii. 8 has a finality which belongs to the Latin and not to the Greek.

The Meaning of Faith

"Thy faith hath saved thee; go in peace."

"Believe on the Lord Jesus Christ, and thou shalt be saved."

"I know whom I have believed."

Christianity is fundamentally a religion of salvation. "Christ Jesus came into the world to save sinners." His name was to be called Jesus, for He would "save his people from their sins." It follows that no question can go deeper into the heart of our religion than the question, how does this come about? Both branches of the Church, the Reformed and the un-Reformed, give the same answer, that it is "by faith" on man's side; but they mean totally different things by the word "faith," and the Roman Church adds in effect "and works." If we want to see the difference we have only to compare with the texts quoted above the definite statements of the Athanasian Creed. "Whosoever will be saved, before all things it is necessary that he hold the Catholic Faith." "This is the Catholic Faith, which except a man believe faithfully, he cannot be saved." The difference between believing "on the Lord Jesus Christ" and believing "the whole Catholic Faith" is not a mere difference of language; it represents a fundamental difference between two attitudes of soul.

We need not be surprised to find that there are several meanings attached to the word "faith" in the New Testament. It is the same in English, where we speak of "having faith in princes," "a man of bad faith," "the Christian faith," using the word in three different senses. There is no difficulty in distinguishing these meanings of the word when it appears in the New Testament. Obviously, neither the second nor the third of them has anything to do with the faith that saves. But the first, especially when the idea comes to expression in the form of a word "believe," is itself ambiguous. To "believe in princes" is practically the same thing as to "have faith in princes," yet it is not the same thing as to believe in the law of gravitation or in the Catholic Faith. These we may "believe"; we are not properly said to "believe *in*" them.

We first meet with the words "faith" and "save" in combination when we read the Synoptic Gospels. There are at least four occasions on which our Lord uses the phrase "Thy faith hath saved thee; go in peace." In these passages it evidently belongs to the situation that both words describe an elementary or incipient stage of the condition they refer to. That is to say, we may not read into either of them the full contents of either "faith" or "salvation," as we know them from the rest of the New Testament. The "faith"

47

in each case is something quite inarticulate. It is, in fact, no more than a response to something in Jesus over and above His power to heal or help, a response to something in His character, His sympathy, care and readiness to help or save, a response to the total impression which He makes. He recognises this as "faith," and declares that it establishes a relation with Himself which may issue in something more than the removal of physical need. He "quenches not the smoking wick," but recognises the potentiality of even a minimum of response or self-committal to Himself. We find the converse of this situation in the statement that at Nazareth He could do no mighty works "because of their unbelief." It was not because they did not believe this or that concerning Himself, *e.g.* that He was the Messiah, but because of an entire want of response to the giver on the part of people whose whole mind was set upon the physical gifts which they expected Him to confer. One thing is quite clear, and that is that in none of these cases is there any trace of assent either asked for or given to any proposition however true.

The Fourth Gospel brings abundant confirmation of that interpretation of faith as recognition of Jesus leading to spiritual relation to Him which we find adumbrated in the Synoptic Gospels. In John i. 12 ("As many as received him, to them gave he power to become the sons of God, even to them that believe on his name"), we have the "receiving" of Him treated as synonymous with "believing on his name," that is, believing on Him as known. And a third

48

synonym is added in the same Gospel in the word "know," used in the sense of coming into intimate relation with God or with Christ. "This is life eternal that they should know thee and Jesus Christ whom thou hast sent." To receive Him, to believe on Him, to know Him, these all mean the same thing, and, "he that believeth on me hath eternal life."

"Faith," then, the faith which saves or secures eternal life, is seen in all the Gospels to imply a personal relation to Jesus, a relation of confidence and self-committal to Him as known.

When we pass to the Acts and Epistles it is only natural that we should find the contents both of "faith" and of "salvation" greatly enlarged and enriched. For between the usage of the Gospels and that which we now meet lie the Crucifixion, the Resurrection and the experience of the Living Christ. And now we get such valuations of "faith" and of "salvation" as underlie sentences like, "There is no other name (=person) under heaven whereby we must be saved," and, "By grace ye are saved through faith," and "The life which I now live in the flesh, I live by faith in the Son of God." "Salvation" is now seen to be deliverance from every form of moral servitude, from servitude to Sin, to Fear, to Spirit-forces in the Unseen, to the Law. And "faith" is known to be the going forth of an energy of the human spirit to meet God as He comes to us in Christ, commending His love towards us, offering pardon, peace and fellowship with Himself. It is an act of self-committal to God, in which a man at one and the same time both takes, and gives (himself) and asks. And as it is, in the words of St. Paul, a faith which expresses itself in love (Gal. v. 6), it involves the establishment of a relation between him who has "faith in the Son of God" and the God and Father of that Son. In this relation is found the secret, the motive and the inspiration, of character and conduct which are well-pleasing to God.

This is not to say that this faith through which men are saved is not connected with what may properly be described as belief. It is not faith in a vacuum or a cipher. It is faith in an historical person and in God as revealed by Him. And in order that that person may be known, it is necessary that certain facts regarding Him should be known and accepted as facts. Similarly, the act of faith and the experiences to which it leads invite certain inferences, of which "he died for our sins" is an example. But neither the acceptance of the facts nor the drawing of the inferences is part of the central act of faith, the projection of the spirit of man to meet the saving power of God in Christ. As a writer to the Hebrews puts it, "He that cometh to God must believe that he is, and that he is the rewarder of them that diligently seek him." The "belief" is a condition of the coming, but it is not the coming. "The demons also believe and tremble" (Jas. ii. 19).

This survey of the evidence of the New Testament as to the meaning of faith, the faith that saves, shows a conception which is consistent throughout, with just that difference between the Synoptic Gospels and the other documents which we should expect from the tremendous events which lie between them. There is no need to do more than draw attention to the profound difference between this conception and that which underlies the whole "Catholic" system, and finds classical expression in the Athanasian Creed. "This is the Catholic Faith, which except a man believe faithfully he cannot be saved." There could hardly be a more complete contradiction of the Gospel as we find it in the New Testament. And that it underlies all "Catholic" thinking is shown by the remark attributed to a modern Bishop, "Don't add to the Creed; it only makes it more difficult to believe"; and by what has been written by a distinguished teacher of philosophy, himself an Anglo-Catholic, "otherwise, faith would have lost all its value as a test of man's spiritual condition, and could consequently have no merit towards salvation."

The consequences of this "Catholic" conception of "faith" are seen in some of the other perversions of the Gospel, which must be considered later. But one of them has already come to light in the second of these quotations. Not only is faith described as "a test of man's spiritual condition," it "has merit towards salvation." Nothing could be more directly contrary to the teaching of Jesus, and to that teaching as accepted and expanded by St. Paul. Salvation, or justification, by merit was the root-principle of Pharisaism. The Pharisee in the Parable called God's attention to his "merits"; yet it was not he who left the Temple with a clear conscience in the sight of God. The "works of the Law" which St. Paul repudiated so con-

stantly incurred his criticism not because they were
not, many of them, such as became a religious man,
but because such a man was led to think of himself as
righteous, with a right to claim the favour of God,
through the doing of them. It is this "boasting," as
our English Bible puts it, this "proud claim," which
St. Paul declares to be "excluded" (Rom. iii. 27; iv. 2).
And this is no mere unimportant variation; it goes deep
down into the character of man's relation to God.
Is he a "servant" doing all that he ought to do, and
so "profitable" to God, but in himself complacent,
self-righteous, "despising others," in fact, a Pharisee;
or is he a son serving God as his Father, claiming no
merit or reward beyond the happiness of being well-
pleasing to God.

Grace and Merit

It is difficult for those of us who are reverent students
of words to forgive Roman Catholic theologians
following medieval example for the way in which they
have perverted the significance of the word "grace."
From far back in the Old Testament it had enshrined
a vital and vitalising factor in man's experience of God.
It stood for love in action, love as it radiated from God,
God's love as it reached men in tenderness, mercy and
succour. And its distinguishing quality was that it was
free, unlimited, unconditioned, except in so far as it
was conditioned by a man's being prepared to receive
it. Luke singles it out as that characteristic in the boy
Jesus which was the earliest to receive recognition from
God and from man ("He increased in grace . . . in

the sight of God and man "; Luke ii. 52). John finds in grace coupled with truth or reality the manifestation of the Divine glory of the Son (John i. 14). He represents believers as receiving the whole fullness of Christ in successive waves of grace (i. 16), and finds the essential distinction between the old dispensation and the new in the fact that whereas it was the Law that was given by Moses, what came through Jesus Christ was grace and reality. When we come to Paul we find another who singled out the same quality as characteristic of Jesus ("Ye know the grace of the Lord Jesus"), and gives as an illustration of it nothing less than His "emptying" of Himself at His Incarnation, when "though he was rich, yet for our sakes he became poor." And when he prays for a blessing on the Christians at Corinth, it is the grace of the Lord Jesus Christ which he puts on the same level as the love of God and the fellowship wrought by the Holy Spirit.

It is always the same quality which as it issues forth from God and reaches men is called His grace. It is free as the sunshine, unlimited as the air. It could be said of it as the writer to the Hebrews said of the Word of God, that it is living and effective; it does work. Not that it ever is, as Augustine taught (and others after him), "irresistible." That would destroy the personal quality of the relationship between God and man which is established by grace, and involves the free response of man's will to the gracious will of God. But when that response is given, a channel is opened by which man receives successive waves of grace, and discovers that by grace he is being saved, helped, strengthened, inspired. Grace finds its supreme embodiment in Jesus Christ, His Incarnation and His sacrificial death, and he who responds to it with the act and habit of faith finds that that which is essentially universal focuses upon him, his need, his temptation, his task. And the focusing is done by God, without the intrusion of any human agency. For, as Paul rejoiced to remember: "If anyone loves God, the same is known by him."

It was to this Divine grace that the Publican in the parable appealed. The Pharisee appealed to his "works," to the merit which he had accumulated through punctilious observance of the Law. He practically demanded that God would forgive him. He made what St. Paul called a "proud claim" (Rom. iv. 2). But Jesus declared that it was the other man who returned from the Temple with a clear conscience. This meant nothing less than a revolution in a fundamental conception of religion. It was a complete reversal of the Pharisaic theory of justification or salvation by merit. For that theory is not fully described as "legalism." It was the purpose behind, or the promise attached to, this legalism that mattered. It meant that man had power to bring pressure upon God, which in the nature of things He could not resist. It rested ultimately upon a conception of God which was not that of the prophets. Post-prophetic Judaism had seen a steadily increasing emphasis upon the transcendence of God, the substitution of a contractual for a personal relation between God and man.

One of the things which made the religion of Jesus

a new religion was that He magisterially reversed this whole line of thought, taught that men should depend for the forgiveness and fellowship with God not upon a righteousness of their own achieving, but upon the "grace" of a heavenly Father. And part of the indictment against the Roman Church is that it has dared to reverse His teaching, and teach that a man can be saved by his own merit. As the Catholic Dictionary puts it, "God has graciously promised to reward our good works with life eternal." And this is just reproducing the doctrine of the Council of Trent; a man, if already justified, "through such good works as he does by the grace of God and the merit of Christ, whose living member he is, truly merits increase of grace, eternal life, and the actual attainment of eternal life, if he dies in grace."

It is part of the evidence of the harmony between the mind of Paul and that of Christ that he had seized or been seized by this revolutionary principle. His own conversion might be described in a sentence by saying that he exchanged the Pharisee's attitude to God for that of the Publican. "Not having mine own righteousness, which is through the law, but that which is through faith in Christ." "By grace ye are saved through faith; and that not of yourselves; it is the gift of God; not of works, lest any man should make a proud claim." It was not without reason that Luther called the Epistle of James an "epistle of straw"; for "James" was probably written during that half-century after A.D. 70 when, as we have seen, the teaching of St. Paul was less known and less regarded than at any other time in the history of the Church. "By works (that is, by merit) a man is justified, and not by faith only." St. Paul's "faith which expresses itself in love" could never be "without works." But James' handling of the subject betrays that return to principles of Judaism which made "reformation" necessary almost from the beginning.

Yet clearer evidence of departure alike from the New Testament and from reason is seen in the Roman doctrine of works of "supererogation." By this is meant, in the first place, the theory that persons of extraordinary saintliness, by the performance of good deeds beyond what is required of them by God, can accumulate a surplus of merit; in the second place, that this surplus or part of it can be transferred to others whose merit (or good works) falls short of what is required; and in the third place, that the Church is the custodian of all the accumulated surplus, and has the power to distribute it to others in such proportion and under such conditions as it sees fit. The picture which this brings before one's mind is that of a deposit bank with branches throughout the world, whose assets are intangible and their amount known to no one. The authorities who manage the bank claim that they bestow upon such persons as they choose spiritual property of inestimable value—what, in fact, can make them safe for eternity. And there are people who have been persuaded to believe in the reality of the capital and in the power of the Church to disburse it, and who even in some cases give solid cash in return.

Once more we see in this assertion of merit as a

means of obtaining grace nothing less than the revival or survival of a governing idea of later Judaism. We find it in 1 Clement, "justified by works not by words," and in 2 Clement, "fasting is better than prayer, but the giving of alms is better than both"; "almsgiving is something that lightens sin." So also the idea that the surplus merit of one man can be transferred to the credit of another goes back to the post-exilic literature of the Jews.

All this represents a fundamental perversion of the Gospel, the seriousness of which can hardly be exaggerated. It stands for a return to the pre-Christian contractual relation to God, that of a servant or a slave. It tacitly denies the relation of sonship which is opened to men through Christ. Again, we point out how deeply this experience has entered into the consciousness of St. Paul. We hear the expression of his triumphant thankfulness in "We are not under the law but under grace," his explanation in the words, "We have received the spirit of sonship." In the Fourth Gospel Jesus is reported as saying, " Henceforth I call you not servants but friends." The Apostle might have put it, "Henceforth he calls us not servants but sons." The relationship to God which Jesus opens to men is one to which the idea of merit, whether operating before or after justification, is utterly foreign; its introduction is a perversion of the Gospel.

In another but hardly less serious way the Roman Church perverts the meaning and the method of Divine grace. It claims to control through its priesthood the supply of this free and unconditioned gift of

God. God sends His grace as He sends His rain, upon the just and the unjust. Its value to any man depends upon the response he makes to it. The Roman Church, under the guidance of its theologians, has analysed this universal gift into various categories, such as the grace of forgiveness or the grace of orders, or sacramental grace. And it is the priest who presides over the distribution of grace in any of its forms. His intrusion between God and man is not only a perversion of the Gospel, it is a challenge to the prerogative of God.

CHRIST IN THE EARLY AND MEDIEVAL CHURCH

WE are approaching the subject of Mariolatry, the position and influence which the Roman Church assigns to the Mother of Jesus. There is no other point at which "Catholicism" so conspicuously departs from Christianity as we discover it in the New Testament. It may be useful, in order the better to understand the rise, growth and predominance of this cult of the Virgin, to consider how much may be accounted for by the conception of Christ which prevailed in the early and the medieval Church. Once more, it is something for which many people are quite unprepared.

Christianity early attracted the attention and ultimately secured the allegiance of several very different classes of men. Christ, in fact, made a very diverse appeal. By no means all of those who became Christians did so because, profoundly conscious of their separation from God through sin, and alarmed at the expectation of judgement to come, they found in the Crucified One forgiveness, peace with God and an assured hope for the future. There were many who had been attracted in the first place to Judaism by its possession of an ancient and noble religious literature, by the many miracles therein recorded and by the high level of morality among the Jews. These found in Jesus the

E* 59

Messiah and in His ethical teaching the fulfilment and culmination of what had attracted them to Judaism and had led them to attach themselves to the synagogue. Another group came from among the "philosophers," men who devoted intellectual power and great earnestness to investigating the mysteries of becoming and being, of the nature of the universe, and of the forces by which it was governed. To men of this type who became Christians the fact of Christ, the Divine Son of God who became man, the Logos who was made flesh, appealed as offering a clue to the problems in which they were so deeply interested. That He became man was an essential part of His value to mankind; but it was on His divine nature that their attention was concentrated, and for a couple of centuries the intellectual power of the Church was wholly devoted to the problems of the relation of the Son to the Father and of the divine and human natures in Christ. For the purpose of such discussions it was sufficient that the human nature, the fact that He was man, was taken for granted. If it had required to be proved, of course the Gospels were there to provide the proof. But as things were, the Gospels were valued only for the evidence they contained as to the foundation-events—the Incarnation, Passion and Resurrection—and for their record of the moral teaching of Jesus.

The result so far as the theologians and official leaders of the Church were concerned was an intellectualised conception of Christ, coupled with an indifference to many features in the portrait of Jesus which are to us of the highest importance and value. There were some thinkers who were actually shy of the Gospel evidence that Jesus was indeed a man, such as His hungering, His seeking for information, even His death, and sought refuge in the assertion that these things were only appearances. But even when this explanation had been rejected, indifference to what we call "the Jesus of history" remained. The Apologists of the second century (Tatian, Athenagoras, Theophilus and Minucius Felix) "display not the slightest interest in Jesus Christ." "In His true manhood Clement of Alexandria is not interested." "The human life of the historic Christ is incomprehensible to Athanasius."

Thus the conception of Christ which is represented by these and other Fathers of the Church is seen to be grievously defective. It takes no account of all that in the Gospels illustrates the true manhood of Christ, the interaction of His manhood with that of other men, His complete acceptance of the conditions of humanity. It ignores those features of His character which are displayed in His understanding sympathy with men and women in various kinds of need, His breaking through ecclesiastical barriers to eat and drink with publicans and sinners, His invitation, "Come unto me, all ye that labour and are heavy-laden," His setting the Kingdom of God before men as embodying an ideal life which is within the reach of all. It ignored all that may be learnt concerning Jesus from His miracles and parables, all that communication of Himself to His disciples which resulted

61

from His intercourse with them. "Thou hast the words of eternal life."

It might be expected that the Reformation, and still more surely the invention of printing with the consequent wide dissemination of the Gospels, would lead to the recognition of this grave deficiency in the medieval portrait of Jesus. But the Reformation itself was followed, so far as theology was concerned, by a period of Protestant scholasticism in which the controversial issues continued to occupy the field, and even the widened circulation of the Gospels did not immediately lead to the discovery of the missing element. The earliest approach to it is found in a Tract on The Aims of Jesus and His Disciples, written by one Reimarus, and published, after his death, in 1778. The situation is thus summed up by Albert Schweitzer: "Before Reimarus, no one had attempted to form an historical conception of the life of Jesus." That in itself goes far to explain the gulf which exists between Romanism and Christianity as we know it to-day.

It is not easy to take in this fact or to do justice to its consequences. But the consequence is nothing less than this, that the "Catholic" conception of Christ was and is (except so far as it may have been modified since the end of the eighteenth century) one which entirely left out what we should call the human or the humane aspects of His character. But it is not difficult to realise that a conception so robbed of all human elements was one which established a great vacuum, or to understand how the vacuum came to be filled, rapidly and almost inevitably, by the Virgin Mary and, in a minor degree, by the Saints.

Nevertheless, this "Catholic" conception of Christ did include certain factors for which New Testament authority could, rightly or wrongly, be claimed. It included and, indeed, emphasised His functions as Legislator and as Judge. He was regarded as a new Moses, and as the Messianic Judge. His precepts bearing on conduct and character were looked on as a New Law, confirming and extending (in one or two instances correcting) the Mosaic legislation. This was, of course, in harmony with the prevailingly legalistic conception of morality which was characteristic of the Jews and especially of the Pharisees. But it was also a natural inference from the form which Jesus gave to much of His ethical instruction. He made free use of the imperative. And it was and is only natural that these precepts should be regarded as "command-ments" and He Himself as a Legislator. Nevertheless, both these inferences are mistaken. Jesus laid down only one "commandment" in the sense of a Divine command applying to all men, in all places and at all times. And that, of course, was, "Thou shalt love." That is to say, He called for a complete reversal of the current of the will in the "natural" man. In so far as that had been directed on the world that passes away, its goods and its values, it was now to be directed towards God with the same interest and affection which had previously been devoted to earthly ambitions and satisfactions. And in so far as in relation to other men personal interest and care for self had been

63

paramount over the interests of others and care for them, the current of will now reversed was to include one's "neighbour" (the man who is thrown across our path), recognised as having claims at least equal to one's own. "Thou shalt care for the Lord thy God; thou shalt care for thy neighbour as thyself."

"On this commandment hangs the whole Law and the prophets." Or, as it is put in John, "A new commandment give I unto you, that ye love one another"; in Paul, "Love is the fulfilling of the Law"; in the First Epistle of John, "Hereby we know that we have passed from death unto life, because we love the brethren." Or, to look at the question in another way, even the Sermon on the Mount does not contain a code of regulations for a world that has not accepted Jesus. That world would, no doubt, do wisely for its own happiness if it did adopt these precepts, or even some of them, and seek to put them in practice. But they are addressed to those who "hunger and thirst after righteousness," who are "seeking the Kingdom of God and his righteousness." That is a righteousness which is spontaneous, and not controlled by law or dictated by fear. It is in this sense that the righteousness of Christ's followers is to "exceed the righteousness of the Pharisees." It is not to "exceed" in fuller contents or in greater perfection, but to be superior to the righteousness of the Pharisees in the spirit in which it is practised. It is to be no longer the outcome of a desire to earn the favour of God, or of fear of penalties, expressing the relation of a bondsman to his master. It is to be the expression of the relation of a

64

son to his father, of one whose delight it is to please God.

If we take the Ten Commandments as a model of what a commandment is, we see that it is precise, of universal application within the jurisdiction of him who commands, and to be interpreted literally. Now most of our Lord's imperatives do not conform to this description. It is not true that they are all to be taken literally. Jesus never spoke more sternly to His disciples than on one occasion when they failed to understand that He was using a metaphor. They had "forgotten to take bread," and when He said to them, "Take heed and beware of the leaven of the Pharisees," they understood Him to refer to literal leaven. In His stern reproach which followed He traced their blunder not to intellectual stupidity, but to "numbness of heart" or "shallowness of faith," really to an imperfect relation to Himself. And indeed there are cases in which no one would think of taking Him literally. As, for example, when He said, "If thine eye cause thee to stumble (lead thee into mischief), pluck it out" (Matt. v. 29). It is a perfectly legitimate use of rhetorical exaggeration in order to convey the appalling nature of the situation. So with, "Resist not evil" and the words which follow (Matt. v. 39). It would be a sufficient reason for not taking the phrase literally that our Lord Himself did not conform to it. At the cleansing of the Temple, whether He did or did not use what could be called violence, He certainly resisted evil in a very public and effective way. So with the words which follow about turning the other cheek, and letting the shirt follow the stolen coat, they refer to such very rare occasions that to take them literally would be to give them very rare application. They are obviously intended to illustrate to the furthest extent the two demands which our Lord most insistently makes upon His followers. The two dispositions or tempers against which He was most anxious to warn men were Vindictiveness and Acquisitiveness. (St. Paul had grasped this teaching: "Avenge not yourselves"; "acquisitiveness which is idolatry.") And what Jesus means is, "Resist not the bad man." Even in the extreme case of an insulting blow see an opportunity (there will be many others) of crushing the impulse to retribution. Even in the extreme case of robbery of the coat you are wearing see an opportunity of waiving your right to your property, asserting to yourself your freedom from the acquisitiveness which sets mankind to work with a muck-rake. Or, as St. Paul interprets this teaching in a sentence that could not be bettered: "Why do ye not rather put up with injury? Why do ye not rather suffer unjust loss?"

Another class of these imperatives is represented by the well-known saying, "Sell whatsoever thou hast, and give to the poor." This doubtless was meant to be taken literally, but it was not a commandment addressed to all the followers of Christ; it was a prescription by the Great Physician for a case in which He had diagnosed the disease, the *dirus hydrops* of acquisitiveness. The prescription was for this sufferer and for all who suffer like him, and it was he of whose need Jesus was thinking, not at the moment of the need of the poor.

There is yet a third class which may be described as Urgent Advice. A good example of this is, "Seek ye first the Kingdom of God."

In general it may be said that many of these precepts are just applications of the one commandment laid down by Jesus. To love God with all one's heart is to crush love of all form of earthly wealth, the spirit of acquisitiveness. To love one's neighbour, to care for his interests even when he is a personal enemy, is to slay vindictiveness.

If we come to the conclusion that it is a mistake, and a serious one, to regard Jesus as a Legislator, as one whose contribution to morality is a new code, we find confirmation in one of His sayings, "Why do ye not of yourselves decide what is right?" That is to say, He threw upon His followers the responsibility, as He opened to them the privilege, of discovering for themselves what was the will of God, always employing, of course, whatever means were available to them for arriving at a just opinion. According to the Fourth Gospel, Jesus promised that the Holy Spirit, who was to take His place when He went away, would guide them "into all truth," truth not merely as to doctrine, but as to duty. That St. Paul understood and accepted this teaching is clear from his declaration that "Christ is the end of law" (or, of the Law), that "the written code killeth, but the Spirit maketh alive," and by the way in which in Romans xii. 2 he claims for Christians who have the Spirit the power of "ascertaining what is the

67

Will of God, the Noble, the Well-pleasing and the Ideal." This power, though not denied to the individual, is specially claimed for Christians assembled in fellowship in the name of Christ (Eph. iv. 21; Phm. 6). The contrast between the dignity and the independence thus assigned to believers in Christ and subservience to a written code interpreted by an external authority is only too obvious. "Where the Spirit of the Lord is, there is liberty." Christ desires the free obedience of free men. He is not rightly understood as the promulgator of a new Law.

The other aspect of Christ which was emphasised with increasing force was that of Judge. For this there was, of course, authority in the function of the Messiah looked for by the Jews. It would be a mistake if because He accepted the confession of Himself as Messiah we were to read back into that Jewish anticipation characteristics of Jesus as we know Him from the Gospels. The Jews did not look for a Messiah who would be a Teacher, a Mediator or a Redeemer, a moral example or one who would forgive sin. He was to come as a representative of God, a theocratic King, and a Judge, who would vindicate and deliver Israel, while he would condemn and destroy the enemies of God's people. St. Paul, who had accepted the Messiahship of Jesus, recognised this as part of His divine function. "We must all appear before the judgement-seat of Christ." But he recognised also the human aspects of His character, His grace, His courtesy and magnanimity, His purity and disinterestedness, His obedience and heroic endurance. It was a very different

68

situation when these characteristics as well as His sympathy and tenderness towards men in need or sorrow were forgotten, and He stood out before men as the implacable Judge. That the word "implacable" is not too strong to apply to the medieval conception of Christ the Judge is clear from the many stories in which His Mother is appealed to to appeal to Him, in some of which at least her appeal fails. Reference might also be made to the witness of art. During the centuries when the subjects represented in mosaic, fresco or painting and also their general treatment were dictated to the artist by ecclesiastical authority, we may find strange confirmation both of the deficiencies and of the emphases in this medieval conception of Christ. Far the greater proportion of these representations have to do with the foundation-events: Jesus as the Babe, Jesus on the Cross, or Jesus returning to heaven. Few, indeed, by comparison are those like Titian's Tribute-money or Masaccio's frescoes at the Carmine, which depict scenes from our Lord's ministry. But He is also depicted as Judge, and no one who has seen, for example, the fifth-century mosaic above the chancel arch in the Church outside Ravenna will have difficulty in understanding how eagerly Christendom in the Middle Age turned from that forbidding figure of Jesus to His Mother, or how imagination was allowed to endow her with those characteristics which the Church had so long ignored in Him.

Christ is the centre of the New Testament. He is the focal point of our religion. He collects in Himself the holiness, the love, and the glorious goodness of God. And these He radiates forth to men. On this all the writers of the New Testament (with one possible exception) are agreed. Differ as they may and do in the angle from which they contemplate this Figure, they are entirely unanimous in regarding Jesus Christ as central and as sufficient for all the religious needs of men. He is the "one Mediator between God and man." No other Mediator is required. "Through him we both (Jews and Gentiles) have access by one Spirit to the Father." For a priest there is neither room nor need. He is an intrusion. And when he claims to decide how and when the divine Grace is to reach his brother-man he challenges a fundamental principle in the religion of Christ.

Moreover, it has great significance that our Lord, followed by both St. Paul and St. Peter, attach dominating importance to a personal relation of His followers to Christ, which can only be described by the word "love." In considering this fact we must, of course, eliminate from the word much, very much, that enters into it in our common speech. We have to distinguish between the word as meaning a passion to give and as meaning a passion to get. There is something which we call "love" which is wholly selfish, and there is something to which we give the same name which implies the surrender of self. It is the latter, of course, which Christ manifests in Himself ("he loved me and gave himself for me"), which He looks for, asks for and acknowledges in those who are His. "He that loveth

father or mother more than me is not worthy of me"
(Matt. x. 37; cp. John xv. 9, 12; xxi. 15). St. Paul
makes this the test of true Christianity: "A ban be on
him who loves not the Lord Jesus Christ" (1 Cor.
xvi. 22). St. Peter, writing to Christians scattered
throughout Asia Minor, people who had never looked
on Jesus in human form, quietly takes their love to
Him for granted ("Jesus Christ whom not having
seen, ye love"; 1 Pet. i. 8). And St. John follows up his
proclamation that "God is love" with the reminder
that "he that dwelleth in love dwelleth in God" (1 John
iv. 16).

Many other illustrations could, of course, be given,
but these are sufficient to make clear that the core and
marrow of New Testament Christianity is found in a
personal relation of men to Christ, a relation which is
established by faith, the faith which expresses itself
through love (Gal. v. 6).

This conception of Christianity, which provides the
foundation for all legitimate development in doctrine,
worship and organisation, is at once simple and profound. For centuries before the Reformation it was
overlaid by a Church for which the human nature of
Jesus was a dogma but not a reality, concealed from
men by the intrusion between God and man of an
authoritarian Church, an imposed system of beliefs,
and a piety which tended increasingly to substitute in
the popular estimation the Madonna and the Saints
for God, the Father, Son and Holy Spirit. It was
through the Reformation, not at it, but after it, that
the New Testament conception of Christ was re-

covered, as one who is not only exalted in glory and returning as Judge, but has entered fully into human life, truly shared its sorrow, temptation and pain, truly manifested man as he can be in relation to God.

MARY THE MOTHER OF JESUS

No Protestant Christian would dream of thinking or speaking of the Mother of Jesus except with entire respect and the deepest sympathy. We remember that she was chosen to be the Mother of our Lord Jesus Christ the Son of God, that she found herself addressed by a heavenly voice, saying, "Hail, thou that are highly favoured, the Lord is with thee"; "Thou hast found favour with God," and that the warning which she received, "A sword shall pierce through thine own soul also," was only too surely fulfilled. Whatever of purity, piety and glad acceptance of a mysterious function assigned to her by the providence of God can be predicated of a village maiden in Palestine we gladly predicate of Mary.

But when we take account of all the propositions which the un-Reformed Church lays down concerning Mary, and which every Catholic is held bound to believe, we are filled with nothing less than amazement, and find ourselves compelled to examine what we really know about her, which is, of course, wholly contained in the Synoptic Gospels, together with one allusion in Acts. And our first impressions may be summed up in, "How very little it is that we know." Indeed, apart from the Annunciation, which is reported by Luke only, the Gospels contain only a few scattered allusions to our Lord's Mother, and of these it is not easy to distinguish the significance. The story of the Annunciation is one of such exquisite beauty and dignity that one shrinks from bringing it into controversial discussion. But it must be said that it falls into three parts: the Salutation (which is repeated), the Promise that Mary shall bear a Son, and the Announcement of the Messianic function and glory which await Him. The first two of these are closely linked together. That Mary has been chosen to be the Mother of the Messiah is the great and sufficient proof that she enjoys the favour (or, has received the grace) of God. "Hail, thou on whom grace (or, favour) has been bestowed; the Lord be with thee." (The words "Blessed art thou among women" do not belong to the original text.) Then in answer to Mary's question. "Fear not, Mary; for thou hast found favour with God." The essential thing is that Mary was chosen for this great function. It is vain for us to try to penetrate to God's reasons for choosing her. We may be sure that there was in her nothing to make her unworthy of the call, but it came to her as an ordinary member of the human race, and to argue from the character of her task that she was all her life free from actual sin is to go beyond the record. This idea that Mary was without sin seems to have sprung up in the fourth century; there is no trace of it in either Irenaeus, Tertullian, Origen or Chrysostom. It afterwards hardened into a doctrine.

The doctrines concerning the Madonna which are officially propounded by the Church are these. She was, like our Lord Himself, sinless; she never committed actual sin. She preserved her virginity to the end of life, that is to say, Jesus was her only child. When she died she was translated bodily to heaven. Finally, she was not only sinless during her lifetime, but made immaculate, free from "original sin" from the moment of her conception. It may be said at once that, while the second of these propositions can be supported only by putting an unnatural meaning upon the language of the New Testament, for the other three there is simply no evidence whatever, either Scriptural or historical.

Before considering such arguments as are offered by "Catholics" in support of these doctrines, it may be useful here to draw attention to the fact that the Roman Church is bound hand and foot to the doctrine of the verbal inspiration of Scripture, and so to interpretations of many Scripture passages which unbiased modern scholarship can only describe as "antiquated." The traditional opening of the defence of these doctrines about Mary provides a good illustration. It is found, for example, in Newman's famous essay on Development of Doctrine. It begins with an attempt to establish a relation of contrast between Mary the Mother of Jesus and Eve the Mother of the race. Eve had sinned in order to become a mother. Mary had become a mother without sin. Eve had brought ruin on her descendants, Mary had been the instrument of salvation. These ideas in reference to Eve have some foundation in Jewish speculations concerning the Fall; those referring to Mary spring from that supreme exaltation of Virginity which marked the adoption of a Manichean estimate of marriage by the Church of the fifth and subsequent centuries, and a desire to credit Mary with something more than merely passive acceptance of the Divine Will. Turning from the beginning to the end of the Bible Newman then finds Mary represented in the "woman clothed with the sun, and with the moon under her feet, and upon her head a crown of twelve stars" (Rev. xii. 1), and sees in the dragon or serpent which makes war upon the woman a reference to the serpent in the garden of Eden. There is therefore "reason for thinking that this mystery at the close of the Scripture record answers to the mystery in the beginning of it, and that the woman mentioned in both passages is one and the same, and that she can be none other than Mary." A moment's reflection shows that in this conclusion Newman actually identifies the two women who are otherwise contrasted in the sharpest possible way. And it only requires a reference to some authoritative Commentary on the Apocalypse to discover that in the woman clothed with the sun we have a bit of Jewish mythology derived from we know not where, but adopted by some Jewish apocalyptist as a symbol of the community of ideal Israel set in the middle of many and great dangers, and subsequently adopted by the Christian writer as a symbol of the Christian Church passing through great tribulation to triumphant victory. The effect, if not the purpose, of the use made of these passages is to build up a pre-supposition of Mary as a being essentially different from the rest of mankind. It is, indeed, such a pre-supposition on which these propositions are actually based.

They are successively deduced from it by what is called "logical inference," and no need is felt for Scriptural authority.

That Jesus was "without sin" is the witness of the New Testament, and is consistent with His consciousness of being "the Son," dwelling in unbroken harmony with His Father's will. But in the case of Mary we have neither any such witness nor any such consciousness. Such allusions to her as we do find in the Gospels subsequent to the Annunciation cannot be said to throw any clear light upon her character or upon her relation to her Son. The finding in the Temple ("Son, why hast thou thus dealt with us? Thy father and I have sought thee sorrowing." "How is it that ye sought me? Wist ye not that I must be about my Father's business?"); the saying, "Who is my mother and my brethren?" when His Mother and His brethren are on the fringe of the crowd, asking for Him; the conversation at the marriage-feast at Cana; the effect of these passages is to suggest a certain distance between Mary and her Son, which is hardly compatible with a profound understanding on her part of Jesus and His mission. On the other hand, as we have already observed, her presence at the Crucifixion and our Lord's words commending her to the care of John do suggest that a deep affection united the Mother and the Son. That "Mary the Mother of Jesus" was among the women who, together with His brothers and the Apostles, habitually gave themselves to prayer in the days before Pentecost (Acts i. 14) is perhaps the most significant thing that we are told about her attitude towards her Son. Beyond these allusions we have simply no information, and it is needless to say that they give no ground for claiming that Mary was sinless.

Also from the fourth century onwards the Catholic Church has tenaciously maintained that Mary pre-served a life-long virginity, that Jesus was her only child. For this there is not only no evidence, but evidence to the contrary if the words "brothers" and "sisters" and "brother" are taken in their natural sense. The explanation which has been traditional in the Church, that the words could be used to refer to cousins, or to children of Joseph by a former wife, will hardly commend itself to any who are at pains to look up the passages (Mark iii. 31; vi. 3; John ii. 12; vii. 2-9; Acts i. 14; 1 Cor. ix. 5; Gal. i. 19). In a word, the usage of these words confirms the simple interpretation which it is natural to give to the words of St. Luke when he tells us (ii. 7) that Mary brought forth "her first-born son."

A third proposition concerning Mary which is commonly held by Roman Catholics is that three days after death her body was carried by angels up to heaven, and her tomb was found empty. This is not an article of the faith, but "the Church signifies her belief in this fact by celebrating the feast of her Assump-tion on the fifteenth of August," and further encourages and approves the belief by selecting for lessons during the feast the passage from an ancient writer in which the history of this Corporeal Assumption is given in detail. The feast was not instituted till the seventh

century, and again there is, of course, no historical
evidence whatever for this story, which, like many
others, was engendered by pious but unrestrained
imagination playing round the figure of Mary. It is,
however, worth while to quote the argument by which
Roman apologists support the story as true, as an illustration of the kind of proof which they offer for many
similar stories. "Mary's corporeal assumption into
heaven is so thoroughly implied in the notion of her
personality as given by Bible and dogma, that the
Church can dispense with strict historical evidence of
the fact."

The culmination of this series of propositions concerning Mary is reached in the doctrine of her Immaculate Conception. As to this doctrine, no doubt
can arise that it is part of the "Catholic faith," which
a man is bound to believe if he is to be saved. It was
the subject of a Bull issued by Pope Pius IX in 1854,
after consultation with Catholic Bishops in all parts
of the world. It declares that "the doctrine which
holds that the most blessed Virgin Mary in the first
moment of her conception was—by the singular favour
and privilege granted by Almighty God, in view of the
merits of Christ Jesus the Saviour of the human race—
preserved immune from every stain of original sin, has
been revealed by God, and is therefore to be firmly and
constantly believed by all the faithful." The Bull goes
on to declare that any who presume to think otherwise have "suffered shipwreck as concerning the
faith," and render themselves liable to "the penalties
determined by law" if they dare to make known by

word or writing or in any other external way what they think in their heart.

The first thing we notice is how exactly the tone and attitude towards mankind by which this proclamation is inspired have in recent times been reproduced in the dictatorships which now control the peoples in certain countries of Europe. It is a claim to an absolute authority which reaches even to a man's thinking and denies the rights alike of reason and of conscience. The only difference is that while the totalitarian State threatens penalties which extend to this life only, the Papal dictator threatens consequences which reach out into eternity—upon all who fail to believe this doctrine.

Yet how shall they believe it? It so obviously has to do with something which lies outside the range of the human mind, something for the truth of which no evidence can ever be offered. As with other doctrines of the same type, once it has been formulated, the claim is made that it has always been the belief of the Church. Yet we can mark the beginning of this belief in the Church and trace its growth. It makes no appearance before the fifth century. St. Basil held that Mary had to pass through the purgatorial fire. St. Augustine was among the earliest of the Fathers who thought it possible that she might be an exception to the rule that all have committed sin, but he includes her with the rest of mankind as sharing the corruption of humanity which began with Adam. It is not until the eleventh century that we find an authoritative writer arguing that Mary was "sanctified in the womb." From that

time onwards the question was fiercely debated in the
Roman Church. St. Bernard of Clairvaux "protested
strongly against the belief in the Immaculate Conception as superstitious and opposed to the tradition of
the Church." He was followed by no less an authority
than Thomas Aquinas. And the matter became the
theme of long and bitter disputes between the Francis-
cans and the Dominicans. To the man of ordinary
intelligence who is confronted with this doctrine it
appears to lie beyond the sphere of human knowledge.
No support for it could be found either in Scripture or
in history. Nevertheless, it made way in the Church,
carried upward from the rank and file to the *intelli-
gentsia* on the wave of popular enthusiasm for Mary
which found both expression and confirmation in an
annual Feast of the Immaculate Conception. Step by
step the doctrine came nearer to official recognition,
until in 1854 it was promulgated as part of the "Catholic
faith."

Roman apologists make only faint-hearted attempts
to support this doctrine from Scripture or from a
continuous tradition reaching back to the early days of
the Church. That the doctrine finds no support in the
New Testament is, of course, obvious to every one.
And even what may be called a tradition on the
subject shows no trace of itself throughout the first
three centuries. In fact, the references to Mary in the
Christian literature of this period are singularly few,
and do not go beyond allusion to the belief that she
was the Virgin Mother of the Lord. An exception may
be found in Irenaeus (*circa* A.D. 200), who may be said

to sow the seed of future speculation when he says that "by yielding obedience she became the cause of salvation to herself and to the whole human race." There is no reason to think that her name was mentioned in any of the liturgies of the early Church, no sign whatever that she was the object of any Cult. The earliest indication of such a development is found among certain women in Thrace and Arabia who are included in a list of heretics "because they were in the habit of adoring the Virgin as a Goddess," and offering to her a certain kind of cake. This is significant beyond its apparent importance, because it suggests what from its beginning onwards was one of the most potent influences in the development of Mariolatry was provided by the pagan worship of Magna Mater or the Mother of the Gods, which was widespread over the Middle East before and after the Christian era. The passage from paganism to Christianity was greatly facilitated when it became possible to suggest that the old allegiance to the Great Mother did not require to be given up, but could be transferred to the Mother of Jesus. There is probably some deep psychological reason for this worship of a woman. A recent convert from the Anglican to the Roman Church gave as her reason for passing over, "It is so nice to think that we have a Mother in heaven as well as a Father," and, of course, the ignoring of all the humane characteristics of Jesus referred to in our last chapter created a vacuum which was only too quickly filled by the figure of Mary.

Romanist Apologists are content to claim that this and other doctrines concerning Mary are established by "logical inferences." But logical inferences must have something corresponding to fact to start from. And in this case the starting-point is provided by a single word—*theotokos*. Towards the end of the fourth century this adjective came to be applied to Mary as an honorific epithet, and not long afterwards was solemnly adopted at a General Council, not, however, so much with the intention of defining the status of the Mother as from a desire to proclaim in a terse and unmistakable way the Church's doctrine as to the Son as laid down in the Nicene Creed. For the word means, "She who bore God." We have here, however, another illustration of the inevitable but unfortunate result which followed from the simple transference of the word from the Greek to the Latin tongue. Its natural equivalent in Latin is "Dei genetrix," and in English "Mother of God." Thus the very word which was intended to close the door against inadequate teaching about Christ opened it to extravagant and unjustified glorification of Mary. The point was made long ago by that saintly and orthodox scholar, Bishop Westcott. In conversation with a friend Westcott, demurring to the statement, "Jesus is God," was reminded of the Athanasian Creed. He replied, "That is just where that Creed is so perilous. The Greek was all right; *theos* described nature, but 'God' suggests the whole Person. *Theotokos* he could heartily say, but the Latin, Dei genetrix, sounded almost blasphemous, did it not?"

Yet it was on the estimate of Mary expressed in this word that the whole series of propositions regarding

her was gradually built up by "logical inference."
As an illustration of what this means we may quote
from a modern authority who defends the doctrine of
the Immaculate Conception thus: "The Christian
mind shudders at the thought that she who was to be
the living Temple of God Incarnate should be permitted by God, who could prevent it, to be first the
abode of the devil." This writer would justify the
last four words by referring to the doctrine of Original
or Birth Sin. And it is only because of this belief that
every human being at and from his birth is a sinner
in the sight of God that Catholics cling to the belief
that Mary, even before she was born into the world,
received the Divine grace whereby she was delivered
from the corruption which Adam had entailed upon
his posterity. This doctrine, which had been strongly
insisted upon by theologians from Augustine downwards, was also taken over by the theologians of the
Reformation, and appears in many of the Protestant
Confessions. But modern Protestant theology has no
place for it. Its only foundation in Scripture is provided by a mistranslation of words of St. Paul in
Romans v. 13. The Vulgate, the official Bible of the
Catholic Church, translates the closing words, "in
whom all sinned," and they have been made by
Catholics and Protestants alike to refer to Adam, who
is alluded to at the beginning of the verse. But this
translation is certainly wrong. The correct meaning
is that given in our English Bible, "for that," or more
clearly "forasmuch as all have sinned." It is sufficient
for the Apostle's argument that "all have sinned," and

84

it is a proposition which few will dispute. What he is concerned about at the moment is the origin of death. It is possible that he still cherished the Jewish idea that the descendants of Adam inherited from him a propensity to sin; but there is the widest difference between such a propensity and being guilty of sin and "the abode of the devil" from the moment of birth. Thus the very reason for claiming an immaculate conception for Mary is illusory. Yet Catholics are held bound to believe in "original sin." They are also held bound to believe that in the case of Mary this "original sin" was cancelled in order that she might be qualified to be the Mother of the Son of God.

The effect, if not the purpose, of these assertions regarding Mary was to raise her above the plane of ordinary humanity, and to bring her very near to the line which divides man from God. It was, in fact, so to enthrone her in the imagination of the devout as to make it natural if not inevitable that they should "worship" her. That she either is, or ought, to be "worshipped" as men worship God is consistently and emphatically denied by Roman authorities, Councils and theologians alike. It cannot be said that the Church officially admits the worship of Mary. A distinction is drawn between the "worship" (*latreia*) which may be offered to God alone and the "super-veneration" (*hyper-dulia*) which ought to be offered to Mary, but to her alone in the whole human race. But, in the Roman Church viewed as a whole the distinction is observed only in a formal way. In what may be called the statutory services worship is offered to God alone, the Mass is offered to God alone. But the reality of worship may be present although the form of it may be entirely absent. When "the heathen in his blindness bows down to stocks and stones" it is not the action that matters so much as what prompts it, the mental or spiritual attitude of the worshipper to the being whom he supposes to be represented by the idol. In the case of the heathen it is primarily fear that prompts him, and a desire to move the unseen power to act favourably towards him. The prostration of soul to which this leads is the essence of worship, and there can be no doubt that for the vast majority of Romanists such prostration of soul is the normal attitude towards Mary. It is the attitude which is encouraged by books of devotion, by hymns expressing extravagant sentiments of admiration and confidence, by the threefold repetition three times a day of the Ave Maria; by the existence of innumerable societies and several Orders devoted to her service, not to speak of the presence in every Catholic Church of a Lady Chapel and an Altar of the Virgin.

What most clearly reveals the incredible extent to which this extravagant adoration of Mary is carried is found perhaps in the relation between her and Christ which expresses itself not only in popular estimation but in the writings of recognised "Doctors" of the Church. The Catholic literature of the Middle Age teems with illustrations of the widespread conviction that one of the functions of Mary is to intercede for men with her Son. Of this belief as prevailing among the rank and file many illustrations are given by Dr.

Coulton.[1] They are many of them childish stories, "from which examples," says one of their chroniclers, "it is manifest that this Mother of Mercy does not suffer sinners to perish, but that she will mercifully free from damnation those who turn to her." In twelve of these stories Christ in His severity refuses to pardon, until the Virgin's pleas bring about a change of the Divine Mind. In three others, where direct prayers to God have failed, prayers to the Virgin are successful.

Thus the final step has been taken, not, of course, with official sanction, but by influential writers and not repudiated by the higher authorities. The Mother is placed above the Son, on the simple ground of her motherhood.

One shrinks from quoting from Alfonso de Liguori (A.D. 1750). His language concerning Mary so far outruns what is credible in anyone who shares the Christian faith in God and in Christ. But his book on the *Glories of Mary* has been immensely popular, was formally recommended for Catholic reading by Cardinals Wiseman and Manning, and the Church of Rome has practically approved its teaching by proclaiming its author a Doctor of the Church. Here are some of Liguori's pronouncements. "Mary is the peacemaker of sinners with God." "Mary is our life because she obtains for us the gifts of pardon and of perseverance." "Many things are asked from God, and are not granted; they are asked of Mary, and are obtained." "Mary has only to speak, and her Son performs all." "He who is protected by Mary will be

[1] *Five Centuries of Religion*, i. 138-154.

saved; he who is not will be lost." "At the command of the Virgin all things obey, even God." Yet the Congregation of Rites decreed in 1803 that in all Liguori's writings there is not one word to be found fault with.

It is difficult to write with becoming restraint of an institution which calls itself the Church of Christ (and denies the title to nearly all other Christian bodies) and at the same time tolerates and even approves teaching such as this. The solemn asseveration that this Church neither practises nor encourages the "worship" of Mary is seen to be a quibble. If the assertions of Liguori are true the Church ought to worship Mary. As it is, they represent a heresy more dishonouring to God and more dangerous to men than any of the heresies which Rome persecuted to the death.

The danger to men is a moral one. The substitution of Mary for God or Christ as the one to whom men turn for help or for forgiveness means the substitution of one who makes no moral demand (or only a trifling one) for One from whom men cannot claim succour without being conscious of a summons to a new life. "Ye shall be holy, for I am holy." It is not, of course, that the granting of Divine help is conditioned by human submission to the demand. That is where "grace" comes in. But a God who only gives is not the God revealed to us in Scripture and supremely in Jesus Christ. His godhead is known to us in the fact that He also asks. It is possible that if we knew more about Mary than we do, we might find in her an example, a moving example, of purity and tenderness and patience. And if certain legends about her could be accepted as true, her figure might convey an effective summons to a better life. But even at its furthest extreme the Roman conception of the Mother of Jesus leaves her a human being, and consequently leaves the moral influence of example partial and limited within a very narrow field. There is not in these legends the slightest suggestion that Mary or the thought of her brings any moral pressure to bear on those who seek her help. The reasons for which her favour is granted are such as these: "that he was wont to say the Hours of the blessed Virgin with devotion," "that his custom (that of an infamous knight) was to salute the Virgin daily," that she (a woman of sin) "visited the Virgin Mary daily and caused a Mass to be sung in praise and glory of the same blessed Virgin."

The substitution of Mary for God or Christ as the normal object of adoration and source of help involves a drastic limitation on the ethical scope of religion. And that such a substitution does, in fact, characterise vast numbers of Catholics to-day is beyond doubt. We may take the evidence of an Anglican clergyman, drawn from his experience among Catholic friends on the Continent. "The result of the doctrine of the Immaculate Conception is to be seen in many Roman Catholics, for the focus of their religion is neither God nor Jesus, but Mary. I have been mocked by foreign Roman Catholics for praying to God. They have told me, 'You are wasting your breath; your prayers will only be heard by God if addressed to Him through Mary.'"[1]

[1] *Church Times*, 7th February 1936.

From all this it is, indeed, difficult to resist the conclusion that the cult of the Mother of Jesus is not only a perversion of the Gospel, but the subversion of Christianity. The very last words which the Roman ritual puts into the mouth of a dying man are, "Mary Mother of grace, Mother of mercy, protect me from the foe, and receive me in the hour of death."

THE LORD'S SUPPER

SOME twenty years after the death of Christ St. Paul writing to the Corinthians reminded them of certain things which the Master had done and said "the same night on which he was betrayed." He states that he had received this information "from the Lord," meaning probably that the original source of it was Christ, though it had actually been communicated to St. Paul by earlier disciples, possibly by some who had actually been present on the occasion. In any case, it had been part of the common tradition of the primitive Church. Moreover, the Apostle had already "delivered" or passed on the information to his converts at Corinth. In this quiet way he conveys to us an impression of the great importance which he attaches to "the Lord's Supper." This and the report itself are further confirmed when we find that each of the Synoptic Gospels reports the same occasion, the same actions, and, with certain minor differences, the same words. In all four accounts we find the same words concerning the loaf, or bread, "This is my body"; in all four the cup or its contents is connected with "the covenant"; in two of them with "the new covenant." Two of the accounts report the words, "This do in remembrance of me." The Apostle further attaches great significance to the rite as a witness to "the Lord's death" and to the spirit in which it is celebrated. Have

G*   91

those who partake shown in the sacred common meal which either preceded or followed the actual Eucharist that they "discern the Lord's Body," that they recognise in practice the true oneness of all its members? Or do they "despise the Church of God," that is, do some of them still remember class-divisions, and permit themselves to eat and drink even more than they need while their poorer neighbours have only meagre fare? This is what St. Paul means by "eating and drinking unworthily." It is failure to show forth "the Lord's death" in its power to create a true fellowship, one which is indifferent to distinctions of wealth, rank, or race. St. Paul believes that this spirit has serious consequences. Like the Word of God itself, the sacrament has judgement-power. It is either an odour of death leading deeper into death, or an odour of life leading to fuller life (cp. 2 Cor. ii. 15). It leaves no man as it found him. By his reaction to it he is "judged." That is to say, it is revealed to what class he belongs, to the living or to those who are "perishing." And the same reaction marks a stage of closer approximation (it may be quite imperceptible) to final death or final Life.

The words "Do this in remembrance of me" are certainly not adequately explained as an injunction to commemorate the Lord by a "memorial feast." They mean, rather, "do this in order to bring me to remembrance." The experience which it may foreshadow is the same as that recorded in Luke xxiv., "He was known of them in the breaking of bread." That is to say, He was recognised as present. Many individual

Protestants have denied the Real Presence of Christ in the Sacrament. That is partly because they have allowed themselves to accept the meaning attached to the word "sacrament" by "Catholics." For these it means the elements, the bread and wine. It can be carried about, from the Church to a house. We have to remember that the word properly describes a rite, a doing, a common action, so that we rightly speak of "celebrating the Communion" as something we do in common. And Christ is really present throughout the whole action, not more really present than He is present with His People at all times, but more vividly present because of the means which He has taught us to use in order "to bring him to remembrance." A still stronger reason for disinclination to admit the Real Presence of Christ in the Sacrament is, of course, dread of the development given to the idea by the un-Reformed Church, the insistence that the bread and wine "become" through Consecration the very body and blood of Christ, with all the superstitious ideas and practices which have followed. It is an illustration of the very understandable disposition on the part of many Protestants to put as it were a buffer state between themselves and "Catholicism." But it remains true that "no Protestant Church has ever denied the Real Presence," and the wise Protestant will boldly press forward to occupy the whole of his spiritual inheritance, right up to the well-defined frontier between what is suggested by Scripture and what is only "Catholic development."

There is one other passage (the only other outside

the Synoptic Gospels) in which reference is made to the Lord's Supper. In 1 Corinthians x. 16 the Apostle asks the rhetorical question, "The cup of blessing which we bless, is it not the communion of the blood of Christ? The bread which we break, is it not the communion of the body of Christ?" It will be observed that counting the six cases in the Synoptic Gospels and the four in 1 Corinthians, there are ten in all in which we are brought up against the crucial question of the meaning of the word "*is*." The contention of the Roman Church has all along been, and still is, that it must be understood literally, that it describes an identity, which is established by consecration, between the elements and the body and blood of Christ. The answer of the Reformed Churches to this contention has not been uniform. It has, indeed, been a great misfortune for the whole Reformation movement that Martin Luther continued to accept this interpretation of the word "*is*," and adhered to it so obstinately that from a very early date there has been a division between this which may be called the Lutheran or "Catholic" view and what is known as the "Reformed" or Calvinist view. Yet there can be no doubt that this view which is held by nearly all the Reformed Churches, which are not "Lutheran," is the correct one. This view is that in all the cases where the word occurs in this context the word "*is*" is to be understood as meaning "represents" or "stands for."

There is no need to enlarge upon the manifold and extraordinary difficulties which attach to the other theory, the difficulty, for example, of deciding what

94

body of Christ it is with which the bread becomes identified—His human body, His resurrection body, or what is vaguely described as His Eucharistic body. The considerations of a positive kind are quite conclusive.

(1) It is possible, and indeed extremely probable, that the word "*is*" was not used by Jesus at all. There was, of course, a corresponding word both in Hebrew and in Aramaic. But in speech or writing it was quite commonly omitted, the hearer or reader being left to infer for himself the relation between the ideas on either side of the gap.

(2) This curious linguistic idiom finds a strangely relevant illustration in 2 Samuel xxiii. 17. Three of David's friends hearing him express a strong desire for water from the well at Bethlehem had broken through the host of the Philistines and brought some to him. When David refused to drink it, but "poured it out unto the Lord," the explanation he gave was, "Is not this the blood of the men who went in jeopardy of their lives?" No one would imagine that the king expected these words to be taken literally. Every one understands he meant "this represents the blood." Yet, as a glance at the English Bible will show, not only is the word "*is*" absent from the Hebrew text, but also the word "this." David held the cup in his hand and said, "The blood of the men that went in jeopardy of their lives." And we all understand what he meant.

(3) Another illustration not less remarkable is found in the Jewish liturgy for the Passover, which comes down from very ancient times and is in use to-day. The

95

head of the household is there instructed to take a loaf in his hand and say in Hebrew words which might be translated, "This is the bread of affliction which your fathers ate in the land of Egypt." To take these words literally would obviously be absurd. And there is, in fact, no word "*is*." The translator of this rubric inserts, therefore, for the benefit of English-speaking hearers the word "*as*"—"This is as the bread of affliction," and is perfectly justified in so doing. Similarly, we are justified in rendering the words of Jesus concerning the loaf, "This represents my body," and concerning the cup, "This represents the new covenant in my blood."

(4) This usage is further illustrated by many passages in the New Testament, in which we unconsciously recognise this meaning of the word, without any attempt to take it literally. Many of these are found in the Fourth Gospel, such as "I am the door," "I am the good shepherd." Others, more striking because less familiar, occur in the Epistles. For example, when St. Paul says of Sarah and Hagar, "These women are two covenants" (Gal. iv. 24), every one understands that he means that they stand for the covenants.

In view of these facts it may be confidently maintained that the way in which both the Roman Church and the Lutheran interpret the word "is" in these passages is wrong. The greatest New Testament scholar in Germany to-day (himself a Lutheran) says of the interpretation adopted by the Reformed Churches, "It should never have been disputed."

If we may attempt an explanation of these sacred words in the form of a paraphrase, it might run thus,

"This loaf represents me, as I give myself in sacrifice to be the spiritual nourishment of men." "This cup represents me as I give myself in sacrifice to seal the new Covenant in my blood." The loaf and the cup were to be signs or symbols whereby men would be helped to realise Christ as the Bread of Life, and Christ as the guarantee of that New Covenant, in which the governing clause was, "I will be their God and they shall be my People."

In the other passage (1 Cor. x. 16) the spiritual value of the Sacrament is presented in a somewhat different form. The word translated "communion" does not signify "participation," so that the two phrases do not mean, as many people take them to do, "participation in the blood, participation in the body." The word means "fellowship," and inasmuch as the word "is" has the same meaning as before, "represents," the phrases should be rendered, "The cup . . . does it not represent fellowship in the New Covenant sealed by my blood?" and, "The loaf . . . does it not represent fellowship in the Life of which I am the vehicle to men?"

"He was known of them in the breaking of bread"— known as living and present.

As they partook of the Bread it helped them to realise that He was present, as He had been with His disciples, to nourish the spiritual Life which He had quickened. As they had said, He had "the words of eternal life," the words which bring it to birth. As they drank of the cup they were helped to realise the sacred fellowship which had been constituted and sanctified by His blood, His fellowship with men, and theirs with one another.

It will be observed that no question of the "validity" of the sacrament arises, that there is no suggestion of an actual partaking either of body or of blood. What is meant by "validity" is given in a higher because spiritual form in the reality of the spiritual experience. The Sacrament was, as Augustine saw it to be, "a picture of the word." And the Word in this case may be summed up in, "I am the Bread of Life"; "Ye are come . . . to Jesus the mediator of a new Covenant," a new fellowship between God and men (see Heb. viii. 6-8; xiii. 24).

Support for the literal or "Catholic" interpretation of the word "is" in the phrase "this is my body" has been found in John vi., where no less than four times Jesus declares in slightly different forms but with great emphasis that the condition of obtaining eternal life is that men shall "eat his flesh and drink his blood" (verses 51, 53, 54, 56). It is maintained that we have here John's version of the same teaching as that which lay behind the words which Jesus used at the Last Supper. He reports them not in connection with the Supper, but with the Feeding of the Five Thousand, which is thus used as a kind of illustration of our Lord's power to feed men with "the bread from Heaven." How far this theory may be correct it is not possible to say, but supposing that it is, we are said to have in this passage a kind of commentary on the words of Institution.

The difficulty of this teaching is greatly increased by the fact that it is set in a context of which it can only be said that it conveys with equal emphasis teaching which appears to be entirely contradictory. "He that believeth hath eternal life" (verse 47; cp. 40; iii. 15; v. 24). The same supreme gift is traced in the one group of sayings to believing in Jesus, in the other to eating His flesh and drinking His blood. Many attempts have been made to explain this contradiction. Some have thought that in verses 51-57 we have a deliberate interpolation embodying a later Church tradition; others that both types of teaching were current when the Gospel was written, and the Evangelist himself incorporated them both, leaving it to others to find an harmonious interpretation.

If that be so, the following points call for consideration: (1) No one dreams or ever has dreamt of taking them literally. No one, that is to say, supposes that Jesus was referring to the flesh and the blood which were His as a man. In verse 52 we find that the Jews understood His words literally, and we are inclined to laugh at their dullness of apprehension. The eating of His flesh in a literal sense would be only a little less abhorrent than the drinking of His blood, against which there was not only a natural shrinking but an express prohibition in the Mosaic legislation. "Ye shall eat the blood of no manner of flesh; for the life of all flesh is in the blood thereof; whosoever eateth it shall be cut off" (Lev. xvii. 14). (2) It is clear, therefore, that not even the Roman Church can take these words literally. Even the doctrine of transubstantiation cannot help it here. It is bound to give the words some metaphorical meaning or other. And what that amounts to is that

99

our Lord invites us to accept these four words in the sense which He gives to them. And the clue to that sense may be found in a certain use of the word "eat" which is to us very extraordinary, but which must have been familiar to the Jews. Thus, the famous Rabbi Hillel, practically a contemporary of Jesus, makes the, to us, amazing remark, "Israel have no Messiah, for they have already *eaten him* in the days of Hezekiah." A later Rabbi, possibly anxious to guard against mis-application of Hillel's words, declared, "Israel shall eat two Messiahs."

The suggestion presented by such language is to us so bizarre that it is well to remind ourselves of the wide application which we give to certain words, like "enjoy." We speak of enjoying a good meal and equally of enjoying a Symphony of Beethoven, and use the same word to express two totally different kinds of experience. The meaning of the word is really governed by the context in which it is used. And in this case the very absurdity of a literal interpretation calls for some such word as "enjoy" to give the true meaning of "eat." "Israel has already enjoyed Messiah and all his benefits" (*Emery Barnes*). This passage thus falls into line with several others in the Fourth Gospel. To receive Christ, to believe on His name (i. 12), to believe on Him (iii. 16), to know Him (xvii. 3), to come to Him (vi. 35), to eat His flesh and drink His blood (vi. 54), all have the same result—eternal life. And if the last of these phrases expresses in the extremest form assimila-tion of Jesus as the Nourishment of man's spiritual life, it is in entire harmony with the teaching concerning faith-union with Christ, which runs through this Gospel. "Faith is already 'spiritual eating,' living communion with Christ, real participation in him" (*Dorner*).

That the Sacrament was thus understood in very early days is shown by a striking invocation to Christ which was used at the celebration of the Lord's Supper, and which has survived in the Acts of Thomas, "Come now, have fellowship with us." It was thus that the early Christians raised their prayer to Christ, and this was the hope with which they approached the Lord's Supper. It was with the living Christ that in the Sacrament they had to do. And so it remains. The presence of Christ in the Sacrament (in the rite, not the elements) gives the Christian all he needs. Christ is there, as He is everywhere, only more vividly realised than He is otherwise. He is there to do for His trusting ones all that He ever did for His disciples. He is there to "make them clean" through the word which He speaks to them; to communicate Himself to them, the nourishment of the Life which He has called into being; to interpret life in terms of the Cross and the Resurrection; to reveal the Father; to bestow the Holy Spirit.

Nor is the element of sacrifice lacking. But it is not Christ who is offered up (except in so far as He is one with His people). The sacrificial offering is of His sacred Body, His People. It has been purified by the Word, "sanctified by the Holy Ghost." It presents itself or is presented by its leader with all its members "a holy sacrifice acceptable to God, which is its im-

material worship." And the minister to whom it
falls to guide and inspire such a celebration of
the Lord's Supper has every reason, with the
Apostle, to bless God for "the grace that is given to
him" (Rom. xv. 15).

THE MASS

IT is difficult to find an appropriate word to describe what took place in the upper room. To call it a "rite" or a "ceremony" is to anticipate what the repetition of it became for the Church. In itself it was a meal taken in common, such as Jesus and His disciples had often partaken of together. It was closely connected with the Passover, either as a celebration or as an anticipation of it. On this occasion it had a specially solemn character, partly due to the foreboding of farewell which communicated itself from Him to them, but particularly due to the very significant acts and words of Jesus. It would not be correct to say that He ordained the repetition or reproduction of the observance. He assumed it when He said of the wine "as often as ye drink it." And that the repetition which began with the beginning of the common life of the Church became and remains to this day, in one form or other, the characteristic feature of its worship, is itself striking evidence of the profound religious significance which the disciples felt to attach to this Last Supper. Simplicity and the profoundest religious significance, these were the two things by which it was characterised. And the religious significance might be analysed as Fellowship or Communion, spiritual Nourishment and utter Devotion, placed within the reach of men by the

H   103

fact that Jesus had given, was giving, and was about to give, Himself "for you," or "for many," or "for the remission of sins."

No one who has been present at the celebration of High Mass in a Roman Catholic cathedral can fail to recognise that what he has witnessed is as poles asunder from the Last Supper the record and significance of which we have just examined. This is true whether we compare the two scenes externally or internally. On the one hand the modest simplicity of a common meal; on the other hand, a spectacle of gorgeous magnificence: lights, colours, vestments, music, incense and, what has a strange psychological effect, a number of drilled officiants performing a stately ritual in entire independence of the worshippers. These are indeed spectators, not participants, spectators like those who were present at a performance of the ancient Mystery Cults. We recall that at the Last Supper those who were present were all of them addressed in the words, "Take, and eat this," "Drink ye all of it." We recall the words which preceded these, "This is my body," "This is my blood of the new covenant." But in the Catholic Mass these words, on which the whole character of the rite depends, though doubtless they have been murmured by the priest, have been heard by none of the Lord's guests. And if perchance they were heard, the hearers would know that they were not expected to act upon them. The only features which the two scenes have in common are thus slurred over in the Mass. We ask ourselves, what is this that we are watching? We are told that the priest is consecrating the elements, and that the effect of the consecration is to change the Bread and the Wine into the very Body and Blood of Christ, and that the priest is offering them to God as a sacrifice; and it dawns upon us that the true analogue of this scene is not to be found in the Upper Room but in the Temple at Jerusalem. Externally, it is a reproduction complete in nearly every detail of that Jewish ceremony; the magnificence and aesthetic appeal corresponded very closely to High Mass in a Catholic cathedral.

The difference is at least as great when we compare the two scenes as to their internal significance. They appeal (for we have no desire to deny that the Mass does make a powerful appeal) to the quite different parts of our nature. The ceremony of the Mass appeals to the "natural man" (as Sohm says, "The natural man is naturally Catholic"), to his aesthetic sense, his sense of beauty, whether seen or heard, his sense of mystery, to which the inaudibility of much of the service makes its contribution, and that curious sense of pleasure which men find in being relieved of all responsibility. Here is something of tremendous importance which is being done for him, and all he has to do is to acquiesce. There are, of course, and always will be, sensitive souls, not a few who, through long training or a natural inclination to mysticism, find in such a ceremony a door into a kind of ecstasy. But similar experiences are not uncommon in other religions, and may even be paralleled in Nature-religions, or in Pantheism. Wordsworth traces to "those beauteous forms" of Nature which he has described:

> " that blessed mood
> In which the heavy and the weary weight
> Of all this unintelligible world
> Is lightened."

From a religious point of view (and that is what matters) all such experiences must be judged by the ethical reactions which accompany or follow them.

The Lord's Supper (to use the Evangelical name for the rite) appeals to and satisfies a very different part of our human nature. Christ is present as *hospes atque epulum*, to use the old phrase, that is, as the true Host and the true Nourishment. He and His People, those who belong to Him, together "celebrate" the Sacrament. It has been made possible by His death, but the communion or fellowship is with Him as living. His People are not spectators only, but participators. They "feed on Him in their hearts by faith." As John Calvin puts it, "We maintain that the body and blood of Christ are truly offered to us in the Supper in order to give life to our souls; and we explain, without ambiguity, that our souls are invigorated by the spiritual aliment which is offered in the Supper, just as our bodies are nourished by earthly bread. We 'shew forth His death' by realising and manifesting how that death has broken down all barriers, racial or social, and has made us one Body, the Body of Christ." As Bishop Gore once said, "Go and tell men that they cannot have communion with Christ unless they have communion with one another." And we express the response of our hearts to the whole sacramental "action" when we say, either aloud or to ourselves, "Here we offer and present unto Thee, O Lord, our souls and our bodies, to be a reasonable, holy and living sacrifice unto Thee."

We need not carry the comparison any further. Those who "prefer" the Roman Mass are obviously applying, whether consciously or unconsciously, a standard which is not a religious one. Neither is it the standard of history, as recorded in the New Testament. Scottish theology has long recognised three aspects or elements in the Lord's Supper: Commemoration, Communion and Consecration. Of these the Roman High Mass eliminates Communion, is silent about Consecration, and gives an illegitimate direction to Commemoration. It is changed into action directed towards God, for which there is no justification in Scripture; it is used to remind God of the death of Christ and its significance, or, in technical language, to represent to God the sacrifice of Christ, and so to offer "the sacrifice of the Mass."

There is nothing in the word "Mass" itself to suggest that this is its character. It appears to have been used in law-courts as well as in churches, and in connection with other services besides the Eucharist, as a signal for departure. The full formula, "*Missa est*," equivalent to "It is over," was employed at the Eucharist to dismiss first the catechumens, when their part of the service was finished, and then the communicants at the close of the whole service. Then the word for dismissal came to denote the service itself from which the persons in question were dismissed.

THE SACRIFICE OF THE MASS

The Mass as a Sacrifice has an importance equal to that of Mariolatry in defining the character of the Roman Catholic Church, and in moulding the mentality of its members. But in regard to it, Roman apologists put up a more serious defence, claiming for it the direct support of Scripture. It is, of course, to the Old Testament that they appeal, pointing to the fact that we find there a complete sacrificial system ordained as a means of approaching or propitiating God, and further, that the sacrifices there prescribed were not of a spiritual or immaterial but of a material kind. They were in fact "animal sacrifices," sacrifices of living creatures. They further maintain that from a very early point in the history of the Church the idea of a sacrifice was clearly associated with the Eucharist, and that the matter of that sacrifice was the Body and Blood of Christ. Both these arguments call for full examination.

It is, of course, true that the Books of Moses, especially Numbers and Leviticus, testify to the important part played by sacrifice in the Hebrew religion. And in the latest document, belonging to the time of Nehemiah, which came to be incorporated in these Books, we find great stress laid upon a very elaborate system of sacrifices, and minute regulations for their proper performance. The purpose of many of the sacrifices was to express and confirm what was felt to be a friendly relation already existing between either the individual or the nation and God. There was one class, however, which may be described as "propitiatory," the purpose of which was to restore that relation when it had been destroyed by sin. And it is this class alone which the Roman Church claims to have been a "type" of the sacrifice of Christ, of which the Mass is a reproduction.

(1) To take the last point first, "nowhere in the Old Testament do we find a hint that sacrifice is to be regarded as a type of something yet future. Those who offered sacrifice did so because they thought it possessed an efficacy there and then " (*Kennett*).

(2) Nothing can outweigh the fact and the significance of the fact that the whole sacrificial system of the Old Testament was not only criticised but "absolutely repudiated" by one after another of the great prophets of the eighth and seventh centuries. The attack begins with Amos (v. 21 ff.): "I hate, I despise your feasts, and I will take no delight in your solemn assemblies. Yea, though ye offer me your burnt-offerings and meat-offerings, I will not accept them: neither will I regard the peace-offerings of your fat beasts. . . . But let justice roll down as waters, and righteousness as a mighty stream." And the prophet actually goes on to question whether Israel brought sacrifices and offerings to God during their forty years in the wilderness. The argument is: "If you did not offer sacrifices in the wilderness, why should they be necessary now?"

Isaiah follows in the same strain (i. 11 ff.): "To what purpose is the multitude of your sacrifices unto me? saith the Lord; I am full of the burnt-offerings of rams, and the fat of fed beasts; and I delight not in the blood of bullocks, of lambs, or of he-goats."

Micah (vi. 1 ff.) puts the same teaching in dramatic form. He first, in the name of God, arraigns Israel to appear before the Divine tribunal, to which at the same time he summons the powers of Nature to act as assessors. Then follows the Divine remonstrance, "Wherein have I wearied thee?" The effect of this is that the people are stricken in conscience, and the prophet, now speaking in their name, propounds the despairing question, "Wherewithal shall I come before the Lord, and bow myself before the high God? Shall it be with burnt-offerings and yearling calves?" The unspoken answer is evidently "No." Then the offer is raised to "thousands of rams and rivers of oil? Again the answer is "No." Once more the offer is raised— to the highest conceivable level of sacrifice in this kind. "Shall I give my first-born for my transgression?" And with the same answer which is evidently expected, the whole theory of placating God by sacrificing one living creature to secure favour for another receives its death-blow. Then the prophet, once more speaking in the name of God, declares what it is that is to take the place of all such sacrifice, namely, justice, generosity and walking humbly with God.

And finally Jeremiah (vii. 21 ff.), proclaiming as a fact what Amos had suggested by a question, says in the name of God, "I spake not unto your fathers, nor commanded them in the day I brought them out of Egypt, concerning burnt-offerings or sacrifices: but this thing I commanded them, saying, Hearken unto my voice, and I will be your God." It is evidently the view of both Jeremiah and of Amos that animal sacrifices had been no part of the original covenant between God and Israel but a human innovation.

The same repudiation of the sacrificial system is clearly heard in several of the Psalms. "Thou desirest not sacrifice else would I give it thee. The sacrifices of God are a broken spirit: a broken and a contrite heart thou wilt not despise" (Ps. li. 16, 17; cp. xl. 6; l. 8). The two verses which follow these in Psalm l. are held by scholars to be a later addition, designed to correct the prophetic teaching of the previous verse (as is also the passage in Jeremiah xxxiii. 17-22 which serves the same purpose). What has taken the place of all kinds of material sacrifice is, according to the Psalmists, thanksgiving; "let them sacrifice the sacrifice of thanksgiving" (Ps. cvii. 22; cp. l. 14; cxvi. 17).

(3) There are some who would seek to turn the edge of this criticism by stressing the fact that there were two schools of thought in Judaism, the priestly and the prophetic holding diametrically opposite views on this subject, and maintaining that as they both have the authority of the Old Testament, it is legitimate for Christians to make a choice between them, and maintain that an "objective" sacrifice was, and still is, an essential part of the Divinely ordained method of worship. The reply to this, however, is simple and conclusive. Christians have no free choice in the matter. It has been settled for them, by our Lord Himself. As between the prophets and the priests, He indubitably attached His teaching to that of the prophets. Quoting Hosea, He on two occasions reminds His critics of the word of God, "I require mercy and not sacrifice"

(Matt. ix. 13; xii. 7). When He is defining the "weightier matters of the Law," which he blames the Pharisees for neglecting, He all but quotes the words of Micah. These weightier matters are "justice and mercy and loyalty," or as Luke reports the last words, "love of God" (Matt. xxiii. 23; Luke xi. 42). He does not criticise the priestly theory of sacrifice; He simply ignores it. Unless, indeed, He includes it in what He sweeps away in the conversation with the Woman of Samaria: "The hour cometh when ye shall neither in this mountain, nor yet at Jerusalem, worship the Father" (John iv. 21). There could be no sacrificial worship away from Jerusalem. "God is Spirit, and they that worship him must worship him in spirit and in truth" (John iv. 24). That seems to leave room for neither priest nor sacrifice.

Of this, our Lord's attitude to sacrificial worship, we may find an illustration in His attitude to the Temple which was its centre. So far as we know from the Gospels He was never present at any kind of service or ceremony in the Temple. Our English versions give the same name alike to the Shrine in which the sacrifices took place and to the great area at the far end of which the Shrine stood. When we read of His being "in the Temple," the reference is to other parts of the area, what we should call the "unconsecrated" parts, where people congregated for intercourse, instruction or discussion. His own description of it was not "the place of sacrifice" but "a house of prayer" (Mark xi. 13). The absence of any record of our Lord's being present at a Temple service is thrown into relief by the care with which the evangelists record His habitual presence at worship in the Synagogues. Luke tells us that "he entered, as his custom was, into the synagogue" (iv. 16), and there took part in the worship, reading a lesson from Isaiah and expounding it. The worship of the Synagogue consisted of just those elements which make up worship in our Presbyterian Churches: reading of Scripture, prayers, chanting of Psalms and exposition of Scripture, or a sermon. And no form of worship in which our Lord thus habitually took part, the value of which He thus recognised, can be inherently inferior to any other form whatever.

(4) The presence of a synagogue or synagogues in each place which Jesus visited (Josephus tells us that there were four hundred synagogues in Jerusalem alone) testifies to the very important change which had come over the Jewish religion since the Exile. The Jews who had been deported from their fatherland into Meso-potamia, and who, during fifty years or more, learnt to make their home there, discovered that it was possible to carry on the worship of God, and to enjoy all the spiritual privileges that flowed from it, without either Temple or sacrifice. It may have been there and then that "synagogues" began; at any rate, it was not long after the Return from the Exile. Those who returned found the Temple in ruins. And though the leaders were anxious to see it rebuilt, we can gather from the prophecy of Haggai that there was no great enthusiasm for this among the rank and file. Even after the re-building this "Temple of Zerubbabel" failed to establish itself in the confidence of many Jews. It was pointed out

that it lacked several things which had given the old Temple its peculiar sanctity, such as the Ark, the Tables of Stone, the Urim and Thummim and the Shekinah or the "Divine Presence." In this dissatisfaction with the new Temple we may see a further indication of the shifting of the centre of gravity in the Jewish religion from the Temple to the Synagogue, from the sacrificial system to the Law. This would be further accentuated as an ever-increasing proportion of the Jewish nation passed their lives at such a distance from Jerusalem that they could be present in the Temple only very rarely or not at all. So we are prepared for the otherwise amazing fact that when Herod's Temple was destroyed and the sacrifices came to an end for ever, it is difficult to discover that the catastrophe had any serious results for the religion of the Jews. It was already independent of sacrifice.[1]

(5) It is a mistake, therefore, to assume that Jews in our Lord's time such as the Twelve or St. Paul, would inevitably look for some form of material sacrifice as embodying the meaning of our Lord's words and action at the Last Supper. And the Supper itself was not a sacrifice. At the most it was the foreshadowing of a sacrifice. Even if it were a celebration of the Passover, that would not bring it into relation with a sacrifice. The Passover lamb was not a sacrifice in the technical sense, any more than the goat which was understood to bear away the sins of the people on the Day of

---

[1] The conclusion thus arrived at is supported by modern Jewish scholars, *e.g.* Kohler, "the great prophets had recognised that the entire sacrificial system was out of harmony with the true spirit of Judaism."

Atonement was a sacrifice. The goat was dismissed, alive, into the wilderness; the lamb was slain for the purpose of a domestic meal. We must not be misled by Paul's words, "was sacrificed for us," in I Corinthians v. 7. It simply means "slain," as in Acts x. 13. The lamb was not slain in the Temple; no part of it was offered to God, or reserved for the priests. But if there was no sacrificial character connected with the meal itself, certain of the words spoken by our Lord pointed forward to a sacrificial character attaching to His approaching death. In connection with the bread, the words "given for you" (Luke) and "for you" (Paul), and in connection with the wine, "shed for many" (Mark), or "for you" (Luke), do not take us beyond a sacrifice in the general sense of a voluntary surrender of self for the benefit of others. But the words "the new covenant in my blood" (Luke and Paul) and "shed for many for the remission of sins" do introduce the idea of sacrifice in its technical sense; but it is a sacrifice which is still to come, and is only symbolised by the breaking of the bread. Of a real "objective" sacrifice there is in the Last Supper not a trace.

(6) Neither is there any such trace of such an idea in the Christian literature of the first hundred and fifty years. The Epistle of Barnabas (about A.D. 125) gives evidence that the Church was still guided by the teaching of the Prophets in the matter of sacrifice. "The Lord has made plain to us that he needs neither sacrifices nor burnt-offerings nor oblations." Then after quoting, as we have done, Isaiah l. 1-12 and Jeremiah vii. 22, he quotes and elaborates Psalm li. 19, "To us

then he speaks thus: 'Sacrifice for the Lord is a broken heart'; a smell of a sweet savour to the Lord is a heart that glorifieth him that made it." Barnabas, at any rate, knows nothing of an "objective" sacrifice in the Eucharist. So untrue is the confident statement that "the belief in the sacrifice of the altar has prevailed at all times and all places within the Church."

This is really the crucial point in the defence of the Mass as a sacrifice, and calls for careful examination. That there was a time, a considerable period, in the early history of the Church when the celebration of the Eucharist was not regarded as the offering of a sacrifice. is proved along two lines of argument. The first is the evidence from authoritative Christian writers of the period, the second the scornful attacks made by non-Christian writers upon the Christian religion on the very ground that it was a religion which had no sacrifices.

To take the second point first, one of the commonest and most effective weapons in the hands of the pagan critics of Christianity was the accusation that the new religion lacked both altar and sacrifice, which were to the pagan mind elementary and essential features of religion. They sneered at a religion which had none of these essential marks, and drew from the absence of temple, altar and sacrifice the inference that the Christians were "atheists." Still more important is it that the Apologists in the second half of the second century, replying to these attacks, did not explain that these critics were mistaken, that the Christians had an altar, though not one for burnt-offerings; that they *did*, in their Eucharist, offer sacrifice, though not of a material kind. There is no suggestion of any such defence. On the contrary, the Apologists justified the absence of these things. They took up the position of the Old Testament prophets in *their* conflict with sacerdotalism, a position which had been further fortified by the accomplishment of the final sacrifice of Calvary, and by the revelation of man's relation to God as a spiritual one, which was now mediated by Jesus Christ.

Thus, Athenagoras, who flourished towards the end of the second century, wrote: "Those who charge us with atheism have not the faintest conception of what God is; they are foolish and utterly unacquainted with natural and Divine things, and measure piety by the rule of sacrifice. . . . As to our not sacrificing, the Framer of the Universe does not need blood nor the odour of burnt-offerings, nor the fragrance of flowers and incense; but the noblest sacrifice is for us to know who stretched out and vaulted the heavens, and fixed the earth in its place like a centre . . . yet it does behove us to offer a bloodless sacrifice and the service of our reason."

Or, to take another Apologist of the same period, Minucius Felix meets the same accusation with a similar reply, "Should I offer victims and sacrifices to the Lord, that I should throw back to Him His own gift? It is ungrateful, when the victim fit for sacrifice is a good disposition and a pure mind and a sincere judgement. Therefore he who cultivates innocence supplicates God; he who cultivates justice makes offerings to God; he who abstains from fraudulent practices propitiates God; he who snatches man from danger slaughters the most acceptable victim. *These are our sacrifices, our rites of God's worship*; thus among us the most just is the most religious."

The same view is represented by Lactantius, as late as the beginning of the fourth century. "What then does God require of man but the worship of the mind which is pure and holy? It is justice only which God requires. In this is sacrifice, in this is the worship of God." We may well ask whether it is conceivable that if the early Church held any view of the Eucharist in the least degree corresponding to the Roman doctrine of the Mass, these representative men would have used such language as this, or that they would have refrained from meeting the pagans' attacks with an exposition of this doctrine.

Even more important is the fact that in the early patristic accounts of the Lord's Supper which have come down to us, we find the same marked absence of any reference to the sacrificial idea. From the middle of the second century we have two detailed accounts by Justin Martyr as to the manner of celebrating the Eucharist. One of them runs thus: "There is then brought to the president or leader among the brethren bread and a cup of wine mixed with water. And he, taking them, gives praise and glory to the Father of the Universe, through the name of the Son and of the Holy Ghost, and offers thanks at considerable length for our being considered worthy to receive these things. And when he has concluded the prayers and thanksgivings, all the people express assent by saying Amen.

And when the president has given thanks, and the people have expressed assent, those who are called by us deacons give to each of those present to partake of the bread and wine mixed with water, over which the thanksgiving was pronounced, and to those who are absent they carry away a portion."

Justin's second account is practically to the same effect. In the *Teaching of the Twelve Apostles* we have the prayers prescribed for use at the Lord's Supper, and in these the meaning of the bread or loaf is found in the symbolising of Christian unity and of spiritual nourishment. "As this broken bread was scattered upon the mountains, but was brought together and became one, so let thy Church be gathered together from the ends of the earth." "Us hast thou blest with spiritual food and drink and eternal light through thy Child." Neither here nor in Justin is there the faintest suggestion that the Lord's Supper is or contains a sacrifice.

Appeal is sometimes made to the verse in the Epistle to the Hebrews, "We have an altar whereof they have no right to eat which serve the tabernacle," but the answer will be found in Irenaeus, "He wills that we also should continually offer our gift at the altar. The altar therefore is in heaven (for thither our prayers and offerings are directed), and there also is the temple"; or in Thomas Aquinas, "That altar is either the Cross of Christ on which Christ was sacrificed for us, or Christ Himself, in whom and through whom we offer our prayers"; or in Bishop Westcott, "In this, the first stage of Christian literature, there is not only no example of the application of the word *altar* to any concrete,

I   119

material object, as the Holy Table, but there is no room for such an application."

It is natural to enquire when this fatal perversion of the Lord's Supper through the intrusion of the sacrificial idea took place, and to causes which led to it. To take the second question first, there was no one to blame for the beginning of this change. It was due to an inherent weakness of human nature, its innate desire to walk by sight and not by faith, its tacit demand for something "solid" or "real" to support the witness of Christian experience. It is because of these things that "the natural (or unspiritual) man is naturally Catholic." They lead him to substitute the symbol for what it symbolises, to adopt the shadow in place of the reality. There is no little historic significance in the names which were successively given to this rite, the "Lord's Supper," the "Eucharist," the "Mass." The fact that on that last night our Lord "gave thanks," a fact which, as we have seen, was reproduced with great and joyful emphasis by the early Church, led to the closest associa-tion between the Supper and thanksgiving. It came to be known as the Eucharist or Thanksgiving. Now, as we have already observed, those Jews who had accepted the teaching of the prophets saw in thanksgiving some-thing which definitely took the place of sacrifice. They offered to God "sacrifices of thanksgiving," believing that these were the sacrifices which God really required. And the early Christians adopted their point of view and followed their example. Thus, "I also assert that both prayers and thanksgivings, made by those who are worthy, are the only perfect and well-pleasing sacrifices to God" (*Justin Martyr*). "We worship God through prayer, and send up this sacrifice as the best and worthiest after righteousness" (*Clement of Alexandria*). "The Saviour enjoined us to offer offerings, but not those which are made by means of senseless beasts or incense, but by spiritual praise and glory and thanksgiving, and by a spirit of friendliness and benevolence towards our neighbour" (*Irenaeus*). "The bread that is called Eucharist is to us a symbol of sacrifice towards God" (*Origen*). And there is that fine phrase of Tertullian, who speaks of the "noble and costly sacrifice of prayer." So far is it from being true that "the belief in the sacrifice of the altar has prevailed at all times and all places within the Church" that down to the end of the second century any idea of sacrifice connected with the Supper, and language which reflects that idea, has to do either with the sacrifice of prayer or with the offering up of the people themselves as a spiritual sacrifice to God.

This brings us to the second line along which the Church moved towards asserting that the Eucharist contained a material sacrifice. This also involved a perversion of a great and noble conception, namely, that in the Sacrament the church or community, conscious of itself as the Body of Christ, and purified as a sacrifice should be by His Word and Spirit, found opportunity to offer itself to God. This is clearly what is before the mind of St. Paul in Romans xv. 16. And in Romans xii. 1 ("I beseech you . . . that ye present yourselves a living sacrifice holy, acceptable to God, which is your immaterial worship") there is a double reference. One is to the symbolic offering at the Lord's Supper, an offering which was at once corporate and individual, an offering up of Christ's Body, the Church, and of each of the believers who united to form that Body. The other is to the working out in daily life of that which is there symbolised, the "pure worship and undefiled before God and the Father" of St. James (i. 27). St. Peter, writing not to the clergy, but to the Christian community, "strangers scattered throughout Pontus," reminds them, "Ye also are built up an holy priesthood, to offer up spiritual sacrifices acceptable to God," and St. Paul describes the self-offering of Christians as their "spiritual worship." In both cases there is an emphasis on the word translated "spiritual." It means "immaterial," and marks the contrast with the sacrifices of the Jews and possibly with those of the heathen in their external and material character. It tacitly excludes every kind of "objective" sacrifice.

And there are many phrases in early Christian literature and liturgies which find their explanation in this most Christian conception that the Church, the Body of Christ (of which we must never forget that Christ Himself is the Head) is the true sacrifice acceptable to God. In the early centuries the Church found in the Lord's Supper an opportunity of offering this sacrifice. They were helped to this conception by the fact that the bread and wine which were used at the Supper had formed part of their common contributions for the needy members of the flock. These contributions

were made not in coin but in kind. As Bishop Gore
put it, "The table of sacrifice in the early Christian
Church must have looked like what our churches look
like at a Harvest Festival." Thus the Bread and the
Wine were taken from the actual offerings of the
people, and we have it on the authority of Bingham
that "for a thousand years the elements were taken from
the people's oblation." "The mystery of yourselves,"
says Augustine, "is placed upon the Lord's Table."
And again, "This is the Christian sacrifice, the many
become one body in Christ. And it is this that the
Church displays by means of the Sacrament of the
altar, where it is shown to her that in what she offers
she herself is offered."

It is a curious and striking fact that the Roman
service of the Mass still retains indubitable traces of
this, the primitive conception. In the Ordinary of the
Mass the oblation or offering up of the elements takes
place *before* they are consecrated. It is the *un*-conse-
crated Host, the simple bread, which the priest offers
to God, saying, "Accept, O Holy Father, this unspotted
Sacrifice" (immaculata Hostia), and this he offers
"for all faithful Christians living and dead." The
Communion Service in the Book of Common Prayer
provides a perpetual witness to the same theory of the
Sacrament. It contains no oblation whatever of the
consecrated elements. In the prayer for the Church
Militant, which precedes the consecration, offering is
made of "our alms and oblations." After the Consecration and Communion, God is asked "mercifully to
accept this our sacrifice of praise," and the only Scrip-

I*   123

tural and primitive conception of sacrifice in connection with the Lord's Supper comes to expression in the words, "Here we offer and present unto thee, O Lord, our souls and our bodies to be a reasonable, holy and lively sacrifice unto thee." [1]

The chasm between this, the primitive conception of sacrifice in connection with the Lord's Supper and the "Catholic" view of the Eucharist as pre-eminently a propitiatory sacrifice may not seem wide, but beyond doubt it is very deep; indeed it involves a change in the whole character of the Sacrament. Down to the end of the second century the Church stood in safety on one side of this chasm. But, already, under various influences, ideas were being pushed forward which tended to throw over it a bridge. And these influences, the conceptions of God and of His relation to man to which expression was now given, were not of specifically Christian origin. On the one hand there were the influences of Judaism made powerful by the uncritical use of the Old Testament. Devoid of any sense of historical development the Church at that time was faced by the alternative of casting overboard the Old Testament altogether and putting it on the same plane as the New. Marcion and other "heretics" did the former, the "Catholics" did the latter. They put the Mosaic ritual and organisation on the same level of authority with Apostolic teaching and example. The sacrifice of the Temple found its parallel in the

[1] In the revised Book of 1928, which was not authorised by Parliament, the prayer containing these words was moved to a position between the Consecration and the Communion.

"sacrifice of the altar." Vestments, incense and aesthetic impressiveness were taken over from the Jewish ritual into the Christian Church. They were the natural paraphernalia of an "objective" sacrifice. That which had been at best temporary and typical, that which had been "done away" in the perfect work and revelation of Christ, was now revived as though it were permanent and eternal in its value.

The man who completed the bridge over which the Church so disastrously passed was Cyprian, at the beginning of the third century. "The writings of Cyprian mark a new stage in the development of ecclesiastical thought and language. In them the phraseology of the Levitical law is transferred to Christian institutions. The correspondence between the old system and the new is no longer that of the external and the material to the inward and spiritual, but of one outward order to another" (*Westcott*). "Cyprian was the first to co-ordinate a specific sacrifice, namely, the sacrifice of the Eucharist, with a specific priesthood. He was the first to describe the 'Passion of the Lord,' nay, the 'Blood of Christ' and the 'Dominica Hostia' as the material of the Eucharistic oblation" (*Harnack*).

In the Mass, therefore, whether we compare it with the Lord's Supper as it is presented in the New Testament or with the Eucharist of the early Church, we see the suppression of the original features of Communion and Consecration of the worshippers, the transformation of Commemoration into Commemoration before God, and a sinking back to the Jewish theory and practice of objective propitiatory sacrifice—in defiance of Him who said, "I will have mercy and not sacrifice."

THE USES OF THE MASS

One would hardly expect to find Romanism going further in indifference to the "faith once delivered to the saints" and enshrined in the New Testament than in its encouragement of Mariolatry and its doctrine of the sacrifice of the Mass. But there is further and grievous perversion of truth in the purposes to which the Mass is applied, and the value which Catholics are taught to attach to "Masses." These uses of the Mass are suggested and defended by the interpretation which the Church puts upon the sacrificial death of Christ. The Church of Rome is irretrievably committed to the doctrine that what Christ offered upon the Cross was a propitiatory sacrifice, and that the Mass is a repetition of a sacrifice of that kind. The Council of Trent declared that "the sacrifice of the Mass is truly propitiatory, and by means thereof we obtain mercy and find grace in seasonable aid." And that there may be no mistake as to the reason why such a sacrifice was required the Council added, "For the Lord, *appeased* by the oblation thereof, and granting the grace and gift of penitence, forgives even heinous crimes and sins." "Wherefore, the sacrifice of the Mass is rightly offered, not only for the sins, punishments, satisfactions and other necessities of the faithful who are living, but also for those who have departed in Christ, and who are not as yet fully purified."

There are at least two things here which challenge the Christian conscience. The first is that God is "appeased by the oblation" of the Mass, as, by inference, He has been "appeased" by the sacrifice of Christ upon the Cross. By this statement the Roman Church stands committed to an interpretation of our Lord's death, which when stated in popular form provides the worst travesty of the Gospel which is current among its enemies. "The death of Christ was necessary to placate an angry Deity." Or, as Mr. Bernard Shaw puts it, expanding that sentence in his own way, "The tradition of a blood sacrifice, whereby the vengeance of a terribly angry god can be bought off by a vicarious and hideously cruel blood-sacrifice, persists through the New Testament, where it attaches itself to the torture and execution of Jesus by the Roman Governor of Jerusalem." If we Protestants have to cope with such a misrepresentation of the meaning of Christ's death, and of God, in obedience to whom He suffered it, the people to whom we seek to present Christ as One who was "lifted up" in order that He might "draw all men" to Himself, and reconcile them to God, reply, "But what a God, a God of vengeance who requires to be 'appeased'"; and they require only to quote the Tridentine Decree in order to prove that this is the doctrine of the Church.

If it should be said that the same doctrine is found in one form or other in several, if not in all, of the Confessions of the Reformed Churches, the answer is simple. Unlike the Roman Church, these Churches rejoice to believe that the Holy Spirit leads Christian men "into all truth," that the interpretation put upon the death of Christ by theologians of the Reformation was neither infallible nor final, and that "sound learning," which is one of the instruments employed by the Spirit, may have brought or may yet bring the Church to a truer understanding of the mind of God than that which finds expression in these documents. The Church of Rome proclaims the Decrees of Trent to be final and "irreformable." For the Churches of the Reformation, Divine truth is always the same, but man's understanding of it progresses from age to age.

We, therefore, have full liberty, sound reasons being shown, to repudiate the theory that the death of Christ was "propitiatory" in the sense that some of the Levitical sacrifices were propitiatory, required and intended to "appease" an angry Deity. We are at liberty to recognise that the theory rests on a mistaken assumption that St. Paul, in consequence of his early training, must have sought in the death of Christ that of which some Levitical sacrifices were a type. These sacrifices were at no time believed to deal with "presumptuous sins," sins committed "with uplifted hand." The penalty for such sins was that the sinner was "cut off from his people," so that even those sacrifices which atoned for the sins of the "people" were of no avail for him. Christian theologians have to give full weight to the striking statement of Dr. Montefiore, "Deliberate sin could not be forgiven by sacrifice, neither did its forgiveness need sacrifice." But it was with sins of this kind that Paul believed that Christ had dealt through His sacrifice. That sacrifice led to the reconciliation of

sinners for whom even the "propitiatory" sacrifices of the Old Testament were of no avail. We may recognise that the word translated "propitiation" in Romans iii. 25 means "propitiator" (one with power to reconcile), and that the passage therefore falls into line with 2 Corinthians v. 18-20, John xii. 32, 1 Peter iii. 18, and other passages. And we may recognise that in the sacrificial death of Christ that which satisfied the Father was His obedience. As St. Bernard put it, "It was not the death that pleased but the will to die." In those who, by faith, are truly united to Christ, His obedience, the perfect harmony of His will with the will of the Father, could be reckoned as their obedience (Rom. v. 19), so that God could at once forgive those who were not in themselves worthy of forgiveness.

If this be the true interpretation of the value of Christ's sacrificial death, to which the Holy Spirit is leading us, we shall recognise that there is good reason for the spontaneous shrinking of the "adequately Christian" mind from the theory which underlies the Roman Mass, and is daily inculcated on innumerable men by the offering of that "truly propitiatory sacrifice." We should see it to be not only false, but in the highest degree derogatory to God.

It is only with increasing wonder that we realise what the "Catholic" conception of God must be as we consider the various purposes for which the sacrifice of the Mass may be, and is, offered, and the classes of people on whose behalf the offering may be made. The aim or purpose of a Jewish sacrifice was never anything else than religious. Directly or indirectly (through the community) it bore on a man's relation to God. Grievously as the Roman Church has erred in introducing into Christianity an "objective sacrifice," it has gone still further wrong in giving a quite unjustified expansion to the purposes for which the Mass is said to be available. We may recall the words of the Council of Trent. "The sacrifice of the Mass is rightly offered, not only for the sins, punishments, satisfactions and other necessities" of the faithful. We may be pardoned for not being certain as to what is meant by "satisfactions." It looks as though it stood for legitimate desires. And that suggestion is confirmed by the words which follow, "and other necessities." By this can only be meant all the common needs of human life, such as food, shelter, health, possibly happiness. What this declaration means, therefore, is that the sacrifice of the Mass, so far from being limited to a man's need of forgiveness and peace with God, is applicable to, and effective in, the whole field which may be covered by prayer.

Now, for such an extension there is no justification either in Scripture or in history. The doctrine of the Mass has followed the same course of development as the doctrine about the Mother of Jesus. It has grown by successive accretions which began in the pious imaginings of plain people, then commended themselves to persons in authority as popular and as useful for keeping people interested and attached to the Church, and finally received authoritative sanction from Council or Pope. Taken in detail, such developments might be looked on as comparatively harmless. But when we look at these developments in the doctrine of the Mass as a whole, we cannot but see that they involve a definite descent from a higher to a lower form of religion. Distinguished anthropologists have pointed out that the dividing line between lower forms of religion and a higher one is reached when "petition takes the place of rites of impetration." "Petition" means "request"; "impetration" means "procuring by request," taking measures to secure that a request is granted. And those rites of impetration, such as prevail in lower forms of religion, are those by which it is supposed by the worshipper that his request will be secured. The common characteristic of all such rites is that the right words are spoken and the right things done by the right person. In the more primitive forms of religion the person may be the individual who desires some favour of the higher powers; in more developed religions the agent is generally the priest. The Mass, then, is obviously a rite of impetration and as such belongs to a lower form of religion. The theory which lies behind it is that it is possible for the right man employing the right means to bring pressure to bear upon God, and that not only with a view to obtaining forgiveness of sin, but with a view to obtaining "satisfactions" and "necessities." It is one of the hall-marks of the superiority of the Christian religion over Judaism that Jesus revealed God as One who neither could be, nor needed to be, concussed by any such method. He opened to His followers the possibility of a relation to God in which the intrusion of such ideas would be not only unnecessary but impossible. The relation of God as

131

Father to men as children involves the recognition of the truth that "your heavenly Father knoweth that ye have need of these things," and the acceptance of the Lord's summons to "seek first the kingdom of God, and all these things shall be added unto you," coupled with repeated encouragement to use the relationship as a ground for petition. Trustful petition is the very sign-manual of sonship. And its place in Christian thought and life sets our Evangelical religion far above any system which practises rites of impetration. The doctrine and the practice of the Mass alike betray a religion which has dropped to a lower level.

Light is thrown upon the true character of the Mass, including the doctrines of Transubstantiation and sacrifice, by two quotations which are given by Heiler in his *Katholizismus*. The first is from a Jesuit Handbook for Meditation which is put into the hands of students for the priesthood. "The priest has power over the lifeless created thing and over the Creator Himself, and that just when he pleases. One word out of his mouth compels the Creator of the Universe and of Heaven to come down to earth, strips Him of His greatness and hides Him under the form of the Bread. And it is only the smallest effect of his word of power, that he controls the created thing, in that he destroys the substance of the bread and preserves its accidents.[1] But a still greater power is added to this, already so great, in that the priest can apply it to the very greatest and most

---

[1] That this phrase was a commonplace of medieval teaching is shown by its appearance in Chaucer (Pardoner's Tale, 71), where it is turned to scornful use.

exalted creature (*sic*), to the Son of Man, and that in the same way as he applies it to the Bread, only in the reverse direction."

The second comes from a named authority, the Cardinal Archbishop of Salzburg in a Pastoral Letter (1906). "Where even in heaven is there such power as that of the Catholic priest? Once did Mary bring the Divine Child into the world, and behold, the priest does it not once but a hundred, a thousand times, as often as he celebrates. To the priests has Christ handed over the right over His holy humanity, to them He has similarly given control over His body. The Catholic priest can not only make it present upon the altar, shut it up in the tabernacle, take it out again, and give it to the faithful to enjoy, . . . Christ the only-begotten Son of God the Father is thus at his disposal."

These amazing statements must be left to speak for themselves. Three remarks may be made, however. It will not be suggested that these statements are officially approved by the Roman Curia. But they are tolerated, and that within a Church which more than any other is swift to mark errors of doctrine and severe in dealing with those who propagate them.

The Roman Church is, as we have seen, in the habit of appealing to "logical inference" when every other kind of evidence is wanting. The case for the doctrine of the Immaculate Conception is a sufficient illustration. And it would be hard to show that these statements do not follow "by logical inference" from the acknowledged doctrine of the Mass.

In these statements we may find the explanation of

the arrogant attitude which is adopted by many priests of the Roman Church. Few men could cultivate for a number of years the consciousness which thus comes to expression without coming to think of themselves as men endued with supernatural power, and endued with supernatural authority over their fellow men.

These statements, if attentively considered, inevitably recall to our minds certain words of St. Paul, when he spoke of one "who opposeth and exalteth himself above all that is called God, or that is worshipped; so that he as God sitteth in the temple of God" (2 Thess. ii. 4). For they involve nothing less than the de-throning of God; they contain a contemptuous challenge to the Sovereignty and Supremacy of God, the foundation doctrine of the Christian religion.

And they are, as we have said, legitimate inferences from the doctrines of the Mass.

Some of these characteristics of the Mass are gravely accentuated in what are known as "private Masses." These are said by the priest assisted by a server. There is no congregation. All but the last feature of likeness to the Last Supper has disappeared. And if the bread is still broken and the wine still poured, it is not with a view to communion, but as a sacrifice pure and simple. Every Mass (to quote another authoritative description) "is a sacrifice of propitiation for sin, and a means of obtaining all graces and blessings from God." Formally, therefore, every Mass is offered partly for the "whole Catholic Church," but in "private Masses" which are said "for a person or persons" the priest "applies in their interest the more special fruit of the sacrifice." Such Masses are said "for the intention" of an individual, and that means in order to secure for him his desire.[1] It does not appear that he is bound to disclose what that desire is, and by an odd but understandable limitation he is guaranteed against any extension of the benefits of the Mass to others "save with the implied condition that the priest does not intend to interfere with the rights of those who have the first claim." We say that this limitation is "understandable" for the simple reason the person for whose "intention" the Mass is offered has paid for it, and it obviously would not be fair if the benefit accruing to him were reduced through its being shared by others. The "intention" may be "satisfactions" of any and every kind, including such things as the *mariage obtenu* which may be seen sometimes on a votive offering dedicated to a Saint in a French church. The burden of our Lord's teaching was, "Have faith in God." The Roman Church teaches, "Have faith in the priest; he can get you what you want, by offering a Mass. He has power not only with God, but over God."

One would have thought that human pretension could no further go. But Rome makes yet a further and more extraordinary claim. She claims that her power through the Mass extends beyond this life into the unseen world, that she is able to affect the experiences,

[1] In 1936 a Mass was said in a church in Cornwall (Anglican) "with the intention" of the conversion of Scotland from Presbyterianism to Catholicism.

and modify the fate, of countless thousands of people who have passed through the gates of death. In order to understand the nature of this claim it will be well to consider first the Catholic doctrine of Purgatory.

PURGATORY, PENANCE AND INDULGENCES

ACCORDING to the official doctrine of the Roman Church, all those who depart this life fall into one of three classes. The first class, which is very small indeed, consists of those who in their lifetime have been wholly purified of sin. They are understood to go at once to Heaven, to enjoy the vision of God and eternal bliss. The second class, and they are the vast majority of mankind, includes all the heathen, all infants who have died unbaptized, and (according to declarations of official authorities), all self-styled "Christians" who have died outside the Church of Rome. *Extra ecclesiam nulla salus.* All these are "damned," and pass at once into Hell, there to endure eternal torment. Between these two classes comes a third, including the vast majority of members of the Catholic Church, those who, though freed by baptism from "original sin," have incurred the guilt of post-baptismal sin, and have not used the means provided by the Church to obtain purification before their death. This great multitude passes into Purgatory, there to endure the "fires of purification" for an indefinite time. It is an Inter-mediate State, and the claim of the Church and so of the priest to be able to penetrate beyond the veil of death, and there to modify the sufferings of the departed or to reduce their duration, a claim which is admitted by all good Catholics, is the ultimate ground of the unquestioning submission of every such Catholic to his priest. Difficult as it is for us to believe that credence can be given by intelligent and educated men to any such claim, we must learn to accept the fact that many such, together with millions of others, live in dread of Purgatory, and are prepared to pay any price, whether in obedience or in coin, in order to obtain assurance of an earlier escape.

It ought to be said that, though the above is still the official doctrine of the Roman Church on this subject, in recent times efforts have been made by individual Catholic writers and theologians to soften it in more than one direction. The medieval representations of the fiery torments of Hell, whether in sermons, in art, or in literature, are no less offensive to the sentiment of educated Catholics to-day than they are to Protestants. And the attempt is frequently made in unofficial quarters to soften (as is supposed) these pictures by substituting mental and moral pain for physical torment. We may sympathise with these attempts, but the fallacy which underlies them is obviously in the suggestion that mental and moral pain is less terrible than physical. It is only childish to suggest that any lightening of the problem of suffering after death, whether remedial or punitive, can be reached along that line. Similar attempts have been made to soften the doctrine that all infants dying unbaptized are damned to all eternity. The means adopted has been to assert that they go to a special department of Hell, reserved for them and known as the *limbus infantium*. Their sufferings there are represented as less severe than those of others in Hell, but they are eternally cut off from the "vision of God," that is, from heaven. This solution, apart from its being devoid of all authority, is less to the credit of the intelligence, than of the feeling, of those who offer it. For whatever attractiveness it has depends again upon reversing the places of the physical and the spiritual in the scale of values. It does not really clear the character of God.

The idea of an Intermediate State is another of those ideas for which the Catholic Church is indebted to Judaism. It is implied in a passage in 2 Maccabees (xii. 42 ff.), where Judas Maccabaeus makes a collection of money and sends it to Jerusalem to offer sacrifice for the sins of the dead, "Seeing as he did that an excellent reward is reserved for those who sleep in piety, his design was holy and pious, whence he made the propitiation for the dead that they might be loosed from sin." The date of this is about the middle of the first century, and the ideas which it conveys concerning the conditions of the dead, and the possibility of offering sacrifice on their behalf were developed subsequently in the Rabbinic schools, in which the doctrine was that, "Only a few are sure of immediate entrance into heaven; the majority are at their death still not ripe for heaven, and yet will not be absolutely excluded from it. There is, therefore, a middle state, a stage between death and eternal life, which serves for the final perfecting." It will be noticed how closely the Catholic doctrine of Purgatory is modelled on these Jewish speculations.

When we come to the New Testament we find two

passages and two only which may be thought to support the theory of an Intermediate State. They are both in I Peter (iii. 19; iv. 6). They may be regarded as echoes of the Jewish tradition. The writer of the apocalyptic book which bore the name of Enoch had claimed for Enoch that he had visited the under-world of the dead, and proclaimed to those whom he found there a message of hope. The Christian writer, himself deeply concerned about the fate of the departed, comforted himself and others with the assurance that what Enoch was believed to have done had been done by Christ also. On the other hand, there is definite evidence against the idea of an Intermediate State in our Lord's words to the penitent thief, "This day shalt thou be with me in Paradise," and in language used by Paul. He appears to leave no interval between return to consciousness after death and "being for ever with the Lord"; for him to "depart" is to "be with Christ which is far better." There are many who think that there must be moral progress for Christ's people in the life after death. But it is progress in fellowship with the Lord, progress in which there is no pain except the pain of aspiration, and that is balanced by the certainty of ultimate perfection. "His servants shall serve him; they shall see his face."

With any such conception the Roman doctrine of Purgatory is in hopeless contradiction. There is no suggestion that the souls in Purgatory have any fellowship with Christ, any means of grace, any experience except that of suffering by which they expiate those sins which have not been expiated in their lifetime.

They suffer "the pain of loss"; they "understand in a degree previously impossible the infinite bliss from which they are excluded." They suffer also "the punishment of sense"; they are tormented by material fire; and they have no idea how long they may be kept in Purgatory. It would be hard to conceive of a belief which was so groundless, harder still to conceive of any which could be more ingeniously applied to maintain the domination of an arrogant and greedy priesthood over ignorant or half-educated people. For the Roman Church gives authority to its priests to believe and to teach that by the offering of Masses they have power to reduce for a specified individual the length of his confinement and suffering. And, of course, every such Mass has to be paid for. So that Masses for the dead, Masses for the repose of this or that soul, form a veritable gold-mine for the Church.

It does not appear that the experiences of Purgatory are understood to have any effect on the character of those who are imprisoned there. They do not make progress in Christian virtue or in likeness to Christ. They are said to be purified in the fire, but in practice this means that they work off the penalties for sin which remained undischarged at the time of their death. These penalties, so far as they are imposed by the priest, are described as "penances." The Catholic doctrine of Penance which this introduces is a complicated one, neither has it been uniform throughout the history of the Church. It rests ultimately on a misinterpretation of the Greek word which in our Bible is translated "repentance." The exact meaning of this word, in the

Greek, is "change of mind," and in the New Testament it signifies a complete change of attitude towards God, and man, and the world. In that sense Jesus called upon men to "repent." The Greek word in itself conveys no suggestion of regret or remorse, although, of course, when the change involves recognition that the previous attitude was wrong, it is naturally attended by these. The modern significance of the word is largely due to the rendering given to it in the Latin Vulgate, *poenitentia* (*e.g.* Matthew iii. 2, *agite poenitentiam*, "perform penitence"). This leads to the English "penitent," and that again to "penance." And the loss of its original meaning was confirmed when *poenitentia* was said to be derived from the Latin word for "punishment." Thus one of the key-words of the Gospel became a key-word in the priestly theory of Absolution. In the form of "Penance" it can describe either one of the seven Sacraments which the Roman Church asserts to have been ordained by Christ, or the penalty for sin which the priest imposes as a condition of Absolution. The matter is important for many reasons, and specially for the light it throws on the subject of Indulgences.

We may quote from Heiler a concise and clear statement of the whole subject. "Absolution removes heinous sin and eternal punishment in Hell; the soul is restored to the condition of saving grace; but the punishment in this life, to which a righteous God exposes and must expose the sinful man, is not removed. The sinner must undergo his temporal punishment for sin either in this world or in the next, in Purgatory. The severe penances, which the ancient Church insisted on, before it received again sinners into its fellowship of grace, were the means of cancelling these punishments. But it is not only these penances but all good works which are performed by the pious that have the power to extinguish part of these punishments. The simplest way in which one of the faithful can free himself from them is by the Indulgence. In place of severe penance necessary to escape the punishment the Church substitutes one which is slight, trifling, only a symbol of the punishment. The Church supplements this insignificant performance by drawing on the 'treasury of works of supererogation' the superfluous good works of Christ and the Saints, and so secures the provision of a sufficient compensation."

Among the many things which startle us in this description only two can be mentioned. One is the extraordinary claim which the Church makes to have the power to follow the departed soul to Purgatory, and to reduce at its will the period of its suffering there. This may be looked on as an extension of the power which it claims to offer the sacrifice of the Mass for the benefit of the dead as well as of the living. The same Divine Sacrifice which is understood to "appease" God in His anger against heinous sin may be applied also to mitigate the punishment of "venial" sins, breaches of the Church's law, the penance for which has not been discharged in life. Once more Christ is treated as One who does the bidding of the Church; He is made to serve its interests. The second startling thing is that the Church claims the power to apply to the deficiencies of those in Purgatory the superfluous merits of the Saints, the good works which they performed over and above what God required of them—like the Pharisee in the Parable. This theory is based of course upon the doctrine of salvation by good works or merit, which, as we have seen, was so definitely repudiated by Jesus and afterwards by St. Paul; and it involves the further assertion that these works of supererogation, collected into the "treasury" of the Church, may be credited by the priest to the account of whomsoever he pleases. Apart from everything else which can be said against this whole theory, it involves an obvious deception. We have to think of the rank and file of Romanists who, believing that nearly every one who does not go to Hell goes to Purgatory, are in an agony of fear for themselves or for those dear to them, and prepared to pay almost anything in their power in order to reduce the term of their sufferings. One in such distress pays for ten Masses, for a hundred, for five thousand (it has been done), and if he then asks whether all is right now, the only honest answer would be, "I cannot tell; for I do not know for how long you or your friend are doomed to Purgatory, nor do I really know whether the superfluous merits of the Saints are sufficient to meet the deficiencies of those who go there."

We shrink from bringing all this farrago of inventions even for a moment into comparison with the way of Salvation as we find it in the New Testament. "Greater love hath no man than this, that he lay down his life for his friends." "This is the new covenant in my blood." "God was in Christ, reconciling mankind unto

144

himself." "Christ was once offered to bear the sins of many." "Through him we both have access by one Spirit to the Father." One might quote a hundred such passages, which belong to a different world from that which we have been studying. And we cannot but reflect that these inventions (we must call them so, for they have no foundation either in Scripture or in experience) are inspired by two of the most ignoble features in human nature—the lust for power and the greed of gain.

Indulgences, the abuse of which provided the spark which kindled the Reformation, were, in the meaning and application which were at first given to them, less open to criticism. They referred to the penalties and penances imposed by the Church but not yet discharged by living men. And it was quite within the competence of the Church which had imposed a penance to remit it partially or completely on its own terms, and such a remission was known as an Indulgence. It might be granted on terms which varied from joining in a Crusade to making a money payment, or attendance at the dedication of a Church. But when the effectiveness of an Indulgence came, like that of the Mass, to be extended into the next world, not only was the practice exposed to the same criticism as we have found to attach to the propitiatory Mass, but a new and very serious danger emerged. If it were possible, by a money payment or otherwise, to obtain under the name of an Indulgence remission of sins which had been committed, was it not equally possible in the same way to secure immunity from the consequences of sin which might be committed in the future. The vehement protestations of Catholic writers that this was never the official doctrine of the Church may be accepted as true. But it is not less true that masses of people, especially in Germany, came to look on an Indulgence as guaranteeing them against the consequences of future sin, that they were encouraged to think thus by the arguments by which the travelling "pardoners" sought to induce them to purchase the Indulgences. Striking proof of this is found in a petition which was sent to the Pope from an Assembly of Roman Catholic princes held at Nürnberg in 1522. They set forth One Hundred Grievances of the German People, and among them was this, "Licence to sin with impunity is granted for money. More money than penitence is exacted from sinners. Bishops extort money from concubinage of priests." From the same document we learn that the vendors of Indulgences "declare that by these purchaseable pardons not only are past and future sins of the living forgiven, but also those of such as have departed this life and are in the Purgatory of fire, provided only something be counted down. Every one, in proportion to the price he has paid for the wares, promises impunity in sinning. Hence come fornications, adulteries, incests, perjuries, homicides, thefts, and a whole hydra of evil."[1] This is the testimony of a body of Catholic laymen of high rank which was laid before the Pope five years after Luther had addressed to him a passionate appeal to put a stop to this horrible abuse. To both the Catholic monk and the Catholic princes

[1] Littledale, p. 85, quoting Brown's *Fasciculus Rerum*, 1690, i. 334.

the authorities at Rome turned a deaf ear. The Church could not do without the money. And it did not get it all, for the sale of Indulgences in Germany had been farmed out to a firm of bankers in Augsburg, who received fifty per cent. as commission.[1]

In view of these facts will anyone venture to say that there was not a clamant need for reformation, for a return to the truth of the Gospel in order that there might be a root and branch reform of the whole Catholic system? The reform came, though, unhappily for Europe, it was incomplete. The Counter-Reformation not only checked the spread of the evangelical revival, it finally placed France, Italy and Spain under the dominion of the un-Reformed Church. What may now be the interpretation put upon Indulgences by the rank and file of Catholics it is not for outsiders to say. Probably, in England at least, the idea that an Indulgence secures immunity from punishment for future sin is no longer held or encouraged. But that leaves still the fact that Indulgences are still widely offered upon terms of many different kinds, and that they represent the purchase of hypothetical release from some period of suffering in a mythical Purgatory.

Many people are under the impression that Martin Luther burst forth as a full-grown Reformer, making a comprehensive attack upon Catholic doctrine and Catholic institutions. Some are even under the impression that the famous Theses which he nailed to the

---

[1] The name and the reputation of this firm (Fugger) are preserved in our word "pettifogging," even as the word "hoax" witnesses to the popular contempt for the "mass-priest" with his formula, *hoc est corpus*.

church door at Wittenberg in 1517 contained a complete challenge to the Roman system and an equally complete exposition of the Evangelical counter-blast. As a matter of fact, with only two or three exceptions the Theses had to do wholly with this matter of the Indulgences. They were propositions directed against the mischief they were doing to the German people, and the doctrinal suggestions which they conveyed. These propositions Luther announced that he was ready to defend (after the custom of Universities at that time) against all comers. No doubt his mind was already deeply occupied with questions which touched the very foundations of the Roman system, its doctrines and its authority. He was already construing his own spiritual experience of salvation "by grace through faith" into a gospel which reproduced the great lines of New Testament teaching. But it was not till after the posting up of his Theses and after the refusal of Rome to stop the scandal of the Indulgences that he began to launch a general attack upon the Catholic Church as it had come to be. His success was due in part to the fact that many of his contemporaries, men of position and influence, were shocked and alarmed as Luther had been. Like many of the earlier attempts at reform of the Church the Reformation started from a deep and widespread indignation against the moral and practical abuses for which the Catholic Church was responsible, and then proceeded to trace these things to their source in the falsity of many of its doctrines.

SAINTS, RELICS AND MIRACLES

THE Roman Church recognises a very large number of departed persons, men and women, as "Saints." Its attitude to different members of this body and the kind of veneration which it offers to them is by no means uniform, even as the reasons for conferring the title or status are very various. In general, "Saints" may be said to fall into three classes. There is first the class of those historical persons who bear the name, it may be, because of their relation to our Lord, like Joseph and the Twelve Apostles, or because of their conspicuous services to the Church, whether in scholarship, in defence of the faith or in administration; examples of these are St. Basil, St. Augustine, St. Ambrose, St. Thomas Aquinas. However noble their characters may have been, it is not on the ground of saintliness that they have been canonised. Their names are entered in the Church's Calendar. They are commemorated annually on a certain day. But they play no part in the religious life of the Church. And there is no disposition to worship them or to treat them in any way as other than human. The second class, which is not a large one, comprises men and women whose claim to this recognition rests upon their character more than on anything else. They are the Saints of the universal Church, such as Francis of Assisi, Catherine of Siena and Teresa. Without predicating perfection of any of them ("not perfect, nay, but full of tender wants"), but leaving their perfecting till they attain the vision of God, we join with Roman Catholics in thinking that they deserve the grateful veneration of those who come after. Then there is the third class of men and women who have been solemnly canonised and added to the roll of "Saints" by the Church of Rome. That vast collection known as the Acts of the Saints purports to contain the record of their doings and deservings, and of the miracles which they performed or which have been ascribed to their relics. But it must be frankly stated that a very large part of these records is entirely legendary. About the lives of many of these "Saints" nothing is really known. There are even some of them (*e.g.* Philomena and Expeditus, both popular Saints) who in all probability never existed. It is in this third group that we have to look for the Saints who enjoy great popularity either universally in the Catholic Church or locally in different parts of it. The localisation of many of them (and this is true of the local cults of Mary also, like that of St. Mary of Walsingham) throws an important light upon the origin of their cults. These stretch away back to pre-Christian times, when some lightning-riven mountain or some precious spring of water attracted either the fears or the hopes of a primitive people and they conceived it to be the abode of some unseen power, which, if properly propitiated, would do them no mischief, or do them some good. Such people, newly converted and imperfectly instructed, were allowed to continue believing in these parochial deities, provided they allowed them to be, as it were, baptized into the

Christian system. In the regulations for canonisation issued by the Pope (Urban VIII) there is a curious recognition of the right of this kind of popular sentiment to have its way in this matter. He "did not wish to prejudice the case of those who were the objects of a cultus arising out of the general consent of the Church, or a custom of which the memory of man ran not to the contrary." The rumour that the object of one of these local cults had been appealed to not in vain was sufficient to spread the Saint's reputation far and wide, until, like St. Antony of Padua, he came to be accepted by Catholics everywhere.

The history of Catholicism presents this singular law, that dogmatic theory always lags two or three centuries behind the practical reality. A certain condition is produced by the action of general or natural causes; thence, the condition being established, dogma comes in to supernaturalise and consecrate it in a formula which is then assumed to be primitive and divine. Again and again the Roman Church has left fact and habit to create law and dogma, and has limited its own action to condemnation of those who still hold the contrary doctrine, obliging them to recant or keep silent. A striking example of this is given by the history of the dogma of the Immaculate Conception. A later illustration of the same process is found in the way in which one particular Saint, not unknown but totally unregarded, has in recent years sprung into prominence. A pious woman, in great extremity, not knowing why she did it, called upon St. Thaddaeus, one of the Twelve Apostles, and her prayer appeared to be answered. She spoke warmly of her helper, and others followed her example. The circle of those who looked up to Thaddaeus rapidly increased, and there followed a sort of religious mass-epidemic. And to-day there are great numbers of Catholic churches with statues of St. Thaddaeus, all hung round with votive tablets acknowledging help received from him.

As to the "worship" of Saints there is no part of the field we are exploring in which there is a greater discrepancy between the *dicta* of the central authorities and the attitude and practice of ordinary members of the Catholic Church. The recognised authorities, whether Councils or Popes, strenuously deny that the attitude to Saints which is authorised by the Church goes beyond "veneration." But there can be no doubt that the great mass of Catholics approach Saints with something which is hard to distinguish from worship. We remember that all the essentials of worship may be present though there is no use of the word, no express ascription of Divine honour. When a man looks up to a fellow-creature as the dispenser of supernatural gifts, when he claims his help in circumstances in which God alone can intervene, he worships as truly as do the heathen who bows down to wood and stone. Here the line between what is encouraged by the Church and what is practised by the people may be very thin, but carries great significance. The Church recognises the function of the Saints as intercessors with God on behalf of men, and allows petitions to be addressed to them that they will so intercede. The people, ignoring the fine distinction, address their prayers to the Saint, asking for direct help from him. Thus they give to a human being like themselves the trust and confidence, the honour and the homage, which belong to God alone.

Or, to put it another way, the veneration of the Saints carried to this extreme diverts attention from God. It wholly ignores the teaching of Jesus, who was at pains to fix the attention and the faith of men upon God. In Matthew vi. 25-34 He presses this home upon those who listen to Him with illustrations from the fowls of the air and the lilies of the field, and draws the inference, "Your heavenly Father knoweth that ye have need of all these things." "The very hairs of your head are all numbered." By every means in His power He seeks to give men a sense of their immediate dependence upon God. It is a grievous thing in a Church which bears His name that it leads men to place their dependence on other persons and other things.

From a religious point of view it makes all the difference whether three girls lost on a moor call upon St. Antony (as happened lately), or call upon God. For God is character, and His character is at least partially known, and to call upon Him is, at least half consciously, to acknowledge the moral demand which He makes upon us. St. Antony has no known character. He makes no moral demand. All he asks for is some candles at his shrine and some contribution to his box.

The Roman Church invites men to place dependence not only on beings but on things other than God. It encourages them to put trust in Relics, Amulets and Scapulars. This again is a concession to superstitions which have their roots in paganism. The Saints have

153

at any rate been human beings, with characters which in some cases are known to have been saintly. But these are lifeless objects which are believed to have healing or helping power merely because they have formed part of a Saint's body or even because they have been in contact with him. A relic (or relics) of this kind forms part of the equipment of all Catholic churches of any importance. It is solemnly produced before the assembled people on stated occasions. Every kind of solemnity is used to excite their interest and their confidence in the power which is believed to reside in this material object, a power which passes into them when they prostrate themselves before it and kiss it. These are familiar facts, yet they need to be stated. For it seems to us so incredible that a Church which claims to carry on the work of Christ and to communicate His revelation of God to men should abdicate these god-given functions and encourage simple people in such crass superstition. The people are beguiled. God is dishonoured. Men's attention is diverted from Him.

No importance need be attached to the fact (though it is a fact) that in the case of some specially popular Saints what purport to be parts of a single body are far more numerous in the world than a single body could supply. For Catholics have long ago met this criticism by the simple expedient of asserting that contact with a genuine relic can convey its miracle-working power to what was once part of another body. But it is important that there have been relics devotion to which could only be due to morbid imagination. There is in Dr. Coulton's book an example, the record of which he very properly thinks it right to leave in the original Latin. Such things illustrate the Church's failure to use any moral control over the popular imagination in connection with new cults.

As regards Miracles there is a marked difference between Catholics of the rank and file and Protestants of all classes. It has been described by Heiler thus: "For the Catholic Miracle is the dearest child of Faith. Childish faith in the Divine cannot dispense with Miracle any more than with the sacramental symbol. From mouth to mouth the story of some incredible happening passes, rousing astonishment as it goes. Pious and gifted writers collect and publish the stories. Then the 'legend' passes into the trusted book of edification, which childlike and pious people are never tired of reading. Down to our own time such legends form the favourite kind of religious reading, one might say the Bible, of the Catholic world." And the kernel of every such "legend" is a miracle. The mentality of Catholics everywhere is largely moulded by the reading of this kind of literature. The Bible is not used either at home or in school. Its place must be supplied by lives of the Saints and records of the miracles they have wrought, and also, in schools, by drill in many different "devotions" as well as by Bible stories edited to suit a Roman Catholic atmosphere. The result is to produce an attitude towards reported "miracles" which is entirely uncritical, a will to believe that they have happened, upon grounds which are wholly independent of evidence. This tends greatly to facilitate the "canonisation" of Saints. The Church lays great stress upon the elaborate process which leads up to every such canonisation. In any case the process lasts many years, and may even occupy a hundred. Prior to canonisation must come "beatification," and that calls for not only a stringent examination into the character of the person in question, but for proof that at least two miracles have been wrought either by him or by means of his relics. It is claimed that this proof is rigid. But what proof can there be which would satisfy any but an ecclesiastical court, say, that either John Fisher or Thomas More performed two miracles either directly or indirectly? The conviction that they did so (if we admit the reality of such a conviction) does not spring from evidence of facts; it springs from the will to believe.

These matters, the worship of Saints and superstitions based upon factitious miracles, may seem of minor importance compared with the cult of Mary with its endless elaborations and the perverted applications of the Mass. Attempts might be made to excuse these things as comparatively harmless additions to the central doctrines of Christianity. But it must be remembered that it is these things which to a very large extent make up the religious life of nine-tenths of the Catholic world; and, what is yet more serious, that they—Madonna, Mass, Saints and Miracles—together form the cloud of superstitious belief and superstitious observance which obscures the single and sufficient Saviourhood of Christ and the august and sufficient Sovereignty of God. And by "sufficient" we mean wholly adequate to the moral and religious needs of men.

THE CHURCH

WE have good reason to be proud of the right high and
noble conception of the Church which was recovered
from the New Testament by the leaders of the Reformation, and has been passed on to us by authoritative
documents and teachers in the Reformed Churches
since their time. That conception starts by taking
seriously the recognition that the Church is the Body of
Christ, that people are members of it because they are
members of Christ by faith, and that within that Body
there can be no distinction of "order," such as between
clergy and laity, or between various grades of the
hierarchy. "All ye are brethren," and the only
distinctions within the Body are distinctions of function,
according to the gifts of the Spirit which are severally
bestowed upon different men, and the several kinds of
service which they render. "Paul calls Christ the
Church" says John Calvin commenting on 1 Corinthians xiii. 13. "No one can read the New Testament
without being aware of the extraordinary importance
which it assigns to the Church as the fellowship of
believing men and women. The New Testament shows
not the faintest interest in unattached Christians. It
takes for granted that Christ's followers will hold
together" (*H. B. Mackintosh*). It is "in the company
of God's people" that we learn the dimensions of His
love (Eph. iii. 18).

Before passing on to consider the Roman Catholic Church as an Institution it will be well to satisfy ourselves that this conception of the Church does correspond to that which meets us in the New Testament, and that the form of organisation which we find in the Churches of the Reformation are at least legitimate developments of church order as it presents itself there.

We use the word "Church" in at least four different senses, to describe (1) a building used for Christian worship, (2) the assembled Christians who worship there, (3) the totality of such Christians at any particular time, and (4) the totality of such Christians as belong to one nation or accept one particular type of doctrine, organisation and worship. Neither the first nor the last of these is found in the New Testament. Both the others are so found; "the Church which meets at thy house" (Philem. 2); "God hath set some in the Church, first Apostles," etc. (1 Cor. xii. 28).

Who were the people who took this strange step of assembling together at stated times in a private house to engage in worship? Paul describes one of these groups as "the Church of God which is at Corinth," persons who were called to be God's people ("saints"), having been dedicated to Him in Christ Jesus; and at the same time he registers a strange feeling out for fellowship with all other Christians, addressing at the same time "all those everywhere who called upon the name of the Lord," *i.e.* who worship Christ (1 Cor. i .2). The Church was thus a local fellowship and at the same time a universal fellowship. And what was it that brought these people together, on the first day of each week, to worship Christ, or God through Christ? It was their common faith in Him as their Saviour and Lord, their common rejoicing in what He had done for them, and their common desire to discover the will of God. That desire for "togetherness," on which emphasis is laid in the opening chapters of Acts which bears the strongest witness to a common religious experience, may be described as instinctive. But it would be untrue to say for that reason that the Church was "a voluntary association." They were drawn to one another because they were severally drawn to Christ. They met in Him (Eph. iv. 21). The instinct was evoked by the Spirit, so that He was the creator of the Unity which Paul urges the Ephesians to maintain (Eph. iv. 3).

This situation had already been anticipated in the Gospels. Jesus had foreseen that His followers would gather together "in his name," that is to say, in full consciousness of Him as known. The parallel saying of the Rabbis, "Two that sit together and are occupied with the Law, they have the Shekinah among them," bears out the religious character of the gathering referred to. "There am I in the midst of them." We have here the germinal idea of the Church, a fellowship, a body, a unity or society, of men who habitually "call upon the name of the Lord," and realise His spiritual presence in their midst.

Under each of these designations the idea took firmer shape in the thinking of St. Paul. It was "the fellowship Christ," the fellowship called into being by Him. It was (using a figure already current in pagan literature) the Body of Christ. And Paul delighted to trace out this analogy in detail. Each member of this sacred Body had its particular function, and it was through the harmonious co-operation of all the members that the Body made "increase of itself in love." A new ambition and a new inhibition were introduced into human character, the ambition to promote in every possible way the well-being and the growth of this Body and the inhibition of any kind of conduct which would injure it.

So far we have said nothing about organisation. What we have just described is the *life* of the Church. But the life can neither continue to exist nor propagate itself without an organisation of some kind. We can trace the growth of such organisation in the Church as we meet it in the New Testament. In the Gospels we find no instruction on the subject given by our Lord. But it may be said that He left His followers in the charge of the Apostles. We certainly find them in the Acts taking the lead, as was only natural. They had been chosen by the Master that they might be with Him. To them, or to a group including them, He had given authority to declare what was right and what was wrong for His followers (Matt. xviii. 18), to remit sin and to retain it. What would probably go to confirm their authority was the power which these Apostles had to work what were recognised as miracles. This we know not only from the instances recorded in the Acts, but from the claim which Paul makes to have wrought "the signs of an apostle, in signs and wonders and mighty deeds" (cp. Rom. xv. 19), a claim which he could not have made in the circumstances unless it was both true and known by others to be true.

But the Apostles died out, even those outside the Twelve, who had been admitted like Paul to share their title and their authority. Before the death of Paul other classes of persons were being recognised as qualified to offer different kinds of service to the churches and so as exercising a certain authority. Among these we can distinguish two types. There were those who are enumerated in Ephesians iv. 11 (cp. 1 Cor. xii. 28), those whom God had given or "set" in the Church. Their duties are described as the continuous repairing of the sacred Body, the work of service and the upbuilding of the Body of Christ. They probably exercised their gifts without either appointment or election. The community joyfully recognised that certain persons had been endowed by the Spirit with various kinds of spiritual gifts for the benefit of the Church. There is no suggestion that they exercised any authority beyond that which naturally accrued to them through the discharge of valuable services.

It is probable that those who belonged to this first type were itinerant servants of the Church, not attached to a local congregation. And the first difference between them and the second type, the bishops and deacons, was that these were resident members of the local Church. We first hear of the "bishops" when Paul, addressing "the elders of the Church at Ephesus, bids them "take heed to all the flock, over which the Holy Ghost hath made you overseers." And Paul includes "the bishops and deacons" among those to whom he writes at Philippi. It is not until we come to the Pastoral Epistles that we find instructions given as to these officials. Titus is to appoint "presbyters" in every town (i. 5). The qualifications to be looked for in Presbyters or Bishops are set forth (1 Tim. iii. 1-7; Tit. i. 6-9). They have mainly to do with character. The only function which is suggested for them is teaching. Even at this comparatively late stage in the development of organisation there is no suggestion that these officials exercised any specific authority over a community, though that some of them attempted to do so may have called forth the warning which we find in 1 Peter against "lording it" over the congregations.

We come to the same negative conclusion if we examine the cases in the New Testament in which authority is actually exercised. The "leaders" lead, but the authority and the decisions lie with the body of believing people, the Church. So we find it in Acts xv. 12-29. The matter was argued in the presence of the assembled church. The speakers who are named were not all Apostles. The decision was that of the whole body, and the letter was sent in their name. Exactly the same situation is found at Corinth some years later, when Paul (1 Cor. v. 3-5) calls upon the members of the church "assembled in the name of the Lord Jesus" to take the responsibility of excluding from their fellowship one who was a "notorious evil-liver."

What we find, therefore, is that in the period covered by the New Testament, and down to nearly the end of the first century, there is, apart from whatever special authority conferred upon the Apostles, no evidence of authority being conferred upon, or exercised by, individual officials of the churches. Such authority as was required for the well-being of the community was a prerogative of the community itself. There was, indeed, hardly any limit to this corporate authority. The "saints," that is the People belonging to God, were to judge in disputes between Christians, to "judge the world," even to judge angels (1 Cor. v.).

Beyond this point the organisation of the Church, so far as it is reflected in the New Testament, does not go. After the disappearance of the Apostles there is no trace of "authority" being exercised by any officials as officials, or by any class distinguished as the "clergy" afterwards came to be from the laity. It is clear that further development was bound to follow, as indeed it quickly did. It would not have been possible for a great number of autonomous and unrelated congregations either to maintain the purity of the faith or to carry out successfully the God-given task of world-evangelisation. Some *nexus* had to be found, some means of expressing the common mind not only of a local church but of the whole Church. The situation called for a representative man in each congregation, then in each group of congregations. And he was found, pointed out by his ability and his devotion, in one or other of the presbyters who were also known as bishops. And he quite naturally came to be known as *the* Bishop. Subsequently, and especially since the Reformation, other forms of organisation have been adopted. There is that known as Independent or Congregational, which, while clinging to the theory of congregational autonomy, has modified it in practice, by encouraging congregations to associate themselves in Unions,

County and National, for the sharing of responsibility and the preserving of a common mind. A second form of organisation is that known as Presbyterian, which, starting from the idea of the larger Church, regards each local church as inherently part of a greater whole, just as each individual Christian is inherently a member of the Body of Christ. It is a symbol of this fundamental unity that the Church as a Church accepts responsibility for such duties as the Support of the Ministry and the work of Foreign Missions. If it cannot be said that any one of these types can claim to rest on direct instructions given by our Lord or by His Apostles, it is clear that the Independent type, in its theory, stands nearest to the Church type which we find in the New Testament, while the Episcopal or Catholic stands farthest away. We see no reason to admit that any one of these types is the only one which can claim to embody the essential characteristics of the Church of Christ. On the other hand, we do not say that any one of these types is in itself an illegitimate development. But we do say that one of them, that which is known as "Catholic," does inevitably expose its officials to serious moral danger, and that in the Roman Catholic form it has lent itself all too readily to those serious perversions of the Gospel which we have been examining. The danger is one to which we have not given attention commensurate with the importance which Jesus attached to it. The two things in the character of a man as an individual which He most impressively condemned were vindictiveness and acquisitiveness. That in man as a member of His Society which He warned His followers against with equal earnestness was arrogance, any claim to superiority, any attempt to exercise dominion over the brethren. And He foresaw the danger, especially in connection with the Apostles: "He called the Twelve, and saith unto them, If any man desire to be first, the same shall be last, and servant of all" (Mark ix. 35). Again, almost as if He anticipated what was to happen in the Roman Church, He called ten of the Twelve and said, "Ye know that the princes of the Gentiles exercise dominion over them, and they that are great exercise authority upon them. But it shall not be so among you" (Matt. xx. 25). He even deprecated the bestowal or assumption of titles such as Teacher, Master, among His followers (Matt. xxiii. 8). And it would be consistent with a characteristic of His teaching if in giving these warnings He was not so much concerned about the irritating effect of arrogance upon others, as about its disastrous effect upon the character of the arrogant man. Indeed, He includes it in the list of things which "defile a man," that is, disqualify him for fellowship with God (Mark vii. 22).

Paul shows another of the strange correspondences between his mind and the mind of Christ in that, though he claimed no little authority for himself, he expressly repudiates any "dominion" over the faith of the Corinthians (2 Cor. i. 24). He sees, indeed, the same danger crouching at the doors of the Church as that against which Jesus had warned His followers, the danger of personal ambition, leading some of them to seek to dominate the others. How completely the Roman Church has succumbed to this danger, with grave consequences to members of its hierarchy and to mankind, we cannot help recognising when we consider its character as an Institution.

The picture of the Church which presents itself in the New Testament is primarily that of a fellowship or society of men and women who are conscious of being united to one another in spirit because they are severally united to Christ by faith. This society has a sense of corporate authority over its members in matters of conduct, an authority which extends to the excluding of grave offenders. It also exercises a right to decide important questions of Church policy, being confident that it is guided to a decision by the indwelling Spirit of Christ. It has its leaders, beginning with the Apostles, the men who had been personally commissioned by Jesus to preach or proclaim the Kingdom, and who were among those to whom He had given authority to "bind" and to "loose," that is, to decide what was right and what was wrong for His followers. In the method adopted for filling the place of Judas Iscariot we have a symbolic expression for that combination of a sense of corporate responsibility and dependence on the Holy Spirit which was so marked a feature in the primitive Church. Others, such as Andronicus and Junia, a woman (Rom. xvi. 17), and Paul himself, were subsequently included among the "Apostles." The fact that they were thus included shows that the number of Apostles was regarded as flexible, and further, that the function of an Apostle on which most stress was laid was that of a Missionary, a herald of the Kingdom (Matt. x. 7). The idea of an "Apostolic College" governing the Church, which is so dear to "Catholic" writers, is a gratuitous anachronism. The Church at Jerusalem seems to have had a President, but he was not Peter or any of the Apostles; he was James the brother of the Lord.

But there was in this Church-consciousness—which is reflected in the New Testament—a factor lying deep below anything connected with constitution, organisation or authority, ecclesiastical considerations on which attention is apt to be concentrated to-day. And that was the rejoicing sense of being truly the Body of Christ, the new humanity which was moving towards "the perfect man" (Eph. iv. 13), nothing less than Christ completely realising Himself within mankind (Eph. i. 23). (It was the very thing after which the best minds of our own time, whether definitely Christian or not, are eagerly yearning.) It is this which accounts for the sacredness that attached to the Christian society, the paramount duty of every Christian to reverence the Church, to do all in his power to preserve its peace and foster its growth, as well as the grave danger of doing anything to injure it. "He that dishonours the temple of God, him will God dishonour, . . . which temple ye are" (1 Cor. iii. 17).

As we have already seen, a society of which such a consciousness was the life could not have continued to exist, still less to carry out its duty to "make disciples of all nations," without some form of organisation. It was bound to take shape as an institution. But the grave, the tragic, difference between the Church of the New Testament and the Church as it came to be from

M   167

the fifth century onward and as it is presented by the Roman Catholic Church of to-day is the transfer of emphasis from the consciousness of Life to the ecclesiastical organisation which obscures when it does not choke the Life it was meant to preserve. It is, therefore, a matter of not secondary importance that the Churches of the Reformation, whatever individual organisations they have adopted, have rejected the whole hierarchical theory and system, and accepted an organisation of a simple kind, in which there is no gradation of orders, no divisive difference between "clergy" and "laity," and no man is authorised to "lord it" over the brethren. Nothing could show more clearly the profound difference between the "Catholic" and the "Reformed" attitude to the organisation of the Church than the considered remark of a high dignitary of the Anglican Church, "It must be understood that for us the ecclesiastical *is* the religious." Is there *any* ecclesiastical principle which Protestants would dream of classing as "religious"?

THE ROMAN CHURCH AS AN
INSTITUTION

"My Kingdom is not of this world"; this was the irrefragable declaration of Jesus. And Paul, with his strange insight into the thought of the Master, said the same thing in his own way: "The Kingdom of God is not meat and drink, but righteousness and peace and joy in the Holy Ghost." That is to say, the Kingdom as regards its essential character has nothing to do with material things, but only with things of the Spirit.

Had the Roman Church, which claims to be the embodiment of the Kingdom of God upon earth, set itself deliberately to discredit and deny the principle thus laid down by our Lord and reproduced by His Apostle, it could hardly have done so more effectively than it has consistently done through sixteen centuries. Its ruling ambition has been to be, and to be recognised as, a Kingdom of this world.

To these all-significant words Jesus added, "If my Kingdom were of this world, my servants would fight." And throughout the same period the Papacy has confirmed its contemptuous rejection of this principle by encouraging its servants to "fight," sometimes, when occasion served, with material weapons, at all times with the weapons of political intrigue and astute diplomacy. It has been and is, indeed, a political institution exploiting the highest aspirations and the deepest needs of human nature in the interest of human greed and love of power.

Here is the testimony of a modern Catholic, who had long acquaintance with the Vatican. "The experience of members of the Papal Court which I have gained during many years has given me the unshakable conviction that never, never, unto the world's end, are they prepared to renounce worldly power. They will employ every possible means, now public, now secret, now more now less forcible, to put themselves in possession of this power, and that at any price. Not Religion, not Piety, not Christianity, not Theology is the proper interest of the members of the Papal Curia, but the political advantage of a political institution."[1]

The same spirit animating all ranks of the clergy in their relation to the laity and also to their inferiors in clerical rank equally runs counter to the explicit teaching of Jesus. "The rulers of the Gentiles lord it over them, and their great ones exercise authority over them. But it shall not be so among you; but whosoever will be great among you, let him be your servant." And again, "Be ye not called Rabbi; for one is your teacher, and all ye are brethren." Jesus was not considering merely names and titles whose use is regulated by the sense in which they are employed. He was attacking and condemning the very principle of a religious hierarchy which in earlier religions had divided men into two classes, the laymen and the clerics, putting the consciences of the one class under the tutelage of the other. For this He would have His followers

---

[1] Luigi Puecher-Passavalli, quoted by Baron von Hügel.

substitute spiritual equality and brotherly co-operation founded upon their filial relation to the heavenly Father. The introduction of a hierarchical system which defies this teaching at every turn and continually fosters in individuals the very spirit of arrogance and domination which Jesus condemned is another illustration of the antithesis between Catholicism and the Christianity of the New Testament.

The appearance of that spirit, whether in the Church as an Institution or in the individual members of the clergy, was due partly to human nature, partly to a further borrowing from Judaism. Already, towards the close of the first century, we find the writer of 1 Peter feeling it necessary to exhort the Elders or Bishops that they must not "lord it" (he uses the same word as Jesus had done) over God's people (1 Pet. v. 3; Matt. xx. 25). About the same time we find in 1 Clement the introduction of the fateful distinction between clergy and "laity," in which not the least significant feature is the use of that noble title of the Church, the "People of God" (*laos theou*), to describe a class inferior to the clergy. At the same time Clement opens the door to subsequent developments of the hierarchy when he quotes (but mistranslates) Isaiah lx. 17 in support of his plea for life-tenure of office by the officials of the Church: "I will establish their bishops in righteousness and their deacons in faith." Elsewhere he makes it plain that for him, that is, at Rome and at Corinth, the titles "bishops" and "presbyters" describe the same persons; "Let the flock of Christ," he says, "have peace with the presbyters." And, indeed, as late as Jerome,

M*   171

in the fourth century, we have the testimony, "The presbyter is the same as the bishop, and before parties had arisen in religion, the churches were governed by the Senate of the presbyters."

But long before the time of Jerome the movement had begun which led to the setting of one bishop above his co-presbyters, first in a particular congregation, and then in a group of congregations in the same district. When the district expanded into a diocese, we have the "monarchical" Bishop as we know him to-day in those Churches which follow the episcopalian system. The change appears to have begun in Syria and Asia Minor, early in the second century. Ignatius appears to have been a Bishop in the modern sense of the word. It was only slowly, however, that the movement spread to the West, so that "neither in Rome nor in Corinth was there any Bishop in the Catholic sense" till after the middle of the second century.

It was no doubt for obvious practical reasons that Ignatius took every opportunity of urging obedience to the Bishop, though he did not forget what was due to the Presbyters. "Follow the Bishop, all of you, as Jesus Christ followed His Father, and the Board of Presbyters as if it were the Apostles." "Whoever does anything apart from the Bishop and the Presbytery and the Deacons is not pure in his conscience." After what must have been something like a mass-conversion, and at a time when the Church had neither authoritative documents, nor a literature of its own, a policy such as is here set forth was the only one to meet the situation. "Keep your eyes on those who bear office. Listen to them." They were the custodians of an indispensable tradition.

It was left to Cyprian, a century later, to formulate this threefold Order of Ministry as an essential mark of the Church, and to find a basis and a justification for it in the High Priest, Priests and Levites of Judaism. But it fell to the same Cyprian to be the first defender of the Diocesan Bishops against the pretensions of the Bishop of Rome, who began to claim superiority over the Bishops of other Sees, even as the individual Bishop had claimed superiority over his fellow-presbyters. And this superiority, claimed and after a long struggle admitted, paved the way to a claim for jurisdiction, and that again led after fifteen centuries to the formal acceptance of the Pope as Dictator. The history of this ecclesiastical evolution is that of a triple abdication. The Assembly of believers (Acts xv. 22, 25, 28) first remit the authority which resided in the community to a body of Presbyters, and in its turn the body of Presbyter-Bishops (for at first both were one) becomes epitomised in a single person, the *episcopos* by pre-eminence, the Catholic bishop, until such time as this episcopate in its turn abdicates into the hand of the Bishop of Rome, who thus becomes the universal Bishop, the summary and personification of all Christendom.

The struggle which issued in this result was long and bitter. It only ended in 1870. In its first stage it was a struggle between the Bishop of Rome and the Bishops of sees planted in the principal cities of the East, such as Constantinople, Jerusalem and Alexandria. After the separation between East and West it became a struggle between the Popes and the Bishops in the West. The Bishops were prepared to see their independence qualified by Oecumenical Councils, to which they would assign authority to define doctrine and formulate discipline. Of these General Councils some fifteen have been held. But they had no defined constitution, and were summoned only in an emergency. In theory they consisted of the Bishops of the whole Church and were summoned by the Pope, who presided either in person or through his Legate. Other ecclesiastics and theologians were admitted to some of the later Councils, but not allowed to vote. In theory the Councils were infallible. "What God has spoken through the Council of Nicaea," says Augustine, "remains for ever." But, by a strange inconsistency, it came to be held concerning later Councils that their decrees have no binding authority until confirmed by the Pope. And by no means all the decrees of all the Councils have received that confirmation.

It will be seen at once that under these conditions the attempt to give a conciliar constitution to the Church was foredoomed to failure. Some of the Councils were summoned in order to pacify the indignant demand for Reform which from time to time arose from all parts of the Church. But a Council might drag on for years. The Pope or his representatives were always in the ascendant. Many of the Bishops returned home with a sense of complete defeat. And the Council of the Vatican in 1870 only gave formal expression to what had been for long the working principle of the Church, when it transferred to the Pope the infallibility which since the time of Athanasius had been understood to reside in a Council.

What concerns us here is not only the failure to preserve even the figment of self-government for the Church, but still more the entirely worldly ambition which prompted the whole policy, and the intrigues and political combinations to which it owed its success. Can this be the religion of Him who said, "My Kingdom is not of this world"?

This question is only more urgently pressed home when we consider the claim of the Popes to exercise a political sovereignty in Italy and the history of the States of the Church over which he exercised this sovereignty more or less precariously for ten centuries. The area of his rule varied from time to time, but for a considerable time it extended across the centre of Italy from the Adriatic to the Mediterranean. Naturally it involved all the apparatus of an earthly monarchy, including troops, secular officials, and perpetual negotiations or political intrigues necessary to preserve its independence. This temporal monarchy of the Pope only came to an end when the French troops, which had defended Rome for him, were withdrawn in 1870, and the Italian army occupied the city. The Pope then became technically a subject of the Italian King.

The earthly monarchy of the Pope appeared to be at an end. But altogether unexpectedly it was restored in 1929 by the Lateran Concordat between the Kingdom of Italy and the Roman Church, between Mussolini and the Pope. By this was formally ceded to the Pope as a temporal Sovereign the small fraction of Rome known as the Vatican City. It has an area of about a hundred acres and a population of about a thousand. Within its borders the Pope rules supreme, with his own military guards, his own police, his own diplomatic corps, to which most of the nations send their representatives. The Vatican City is even free from Italian import duties, so that a motor car can be bought there for two-thirds of what it would cost across the street in Rome.

The area of the Pope's political sovereignty may be minute, but the sovereignty is complete. And a thrill of satisfaction ran through the whole Catholic world when it was announced that the Pope, the representative on earth of Him who said, "My Kingdom is not of this world," was once more "Pope and King."

To these political privileges were added for the Church a large sum of money and specific guarantees of independence for the Church. On the surface the Roman Church would appear to have made a very good bargain for itself with Mussolini. We do not know and probably never shall know what was the price it has paid. But in the face of recent history it is difficult to suppress the conjecture that the price paid by the Church included a guarantee that neither priest nor prelate in Italy would publicly criticise Fascist policy. Thus, and some of us might think only thus, would be explained the fact to which the Archbishop of Canterbury has drawn attention, that "no Christian voice was heard in Italy to remonstrate against the use of barbarous poison-gas poured out not only on combatants, but on defenceless men, women and children, by which, ultimately, the spirit of Abyssinia was broken and the victory of Italy was achieved." The offer made by Mussolini and accepted by the Church would then be a simple variant on an offer recorded in the Gospels, "All these things will I give thee (the kingdoms of the world) if thou wilt fall down and worship me."

Another feature which the Roman Church took over from Judaism was a consciousness corresponding to intense nationalism, and an attitude of arrogant exclusiveness over against all non-Catholics. These come to expression in Pharisaic Judaism in the saying, "This people who knoweth not the Law are cursed,' where by "the Law" is meant not only the Law of Moses but the interpretation and application which the Pharisees gave to it. The Pharisees made it a charge against Jesus that He "ate with tax-gatherers and sinners," where by "sinners" is meant not wicked persons but those who, because they knew not the Law, were outside the pale, no better than Gentiles because they did not accept the rulings of the Pharisees. Identically the same position was taken up by the Church at a very early stage, and it is a point on which it may be said that Catholic authority has never varied. "Let no one deceive himself," says Origen, "outside this house, that is, outside the Church no one is saved. For if anyone goes out of its doors, he will become responsible for his own death." Cyprian is the author of the saying, "No one can have God for his father unless he has the Church for his Mother." Boniface VIII

(1302) put the theory with perfect clearness, "We declare, define and pronounce that, for every human creature, to be subject to the Roman pontiff is absolutely necessary for salvation." Pius IX (1854) repeated the doctrine in practically the same words. And the exclusiveness which is the natural outcome of this conviction has found expression in our own time in the words of Cardinal Bourne (1926), "To Anglicans who would ask us to join in Morning Prayer or Evensong, we have only one answer to make, the answer of the blessed Martyr, Margaret Clitherow, 'I will not pray with you, nor shall you pray with me; neither will I say Amen to your prayers, nor shall you say it to mine.'"

One cannot but ask, could Catholics go further in indifference alike to the example and to the teaching of Jesus, reproduced as it is in the example and teaching of His Apostle? He deliberately incurred the hostility of the Pharisees by consorting with those whom they regarded as beyond hope of salvation. It was this spirit of religious complacency and arrogance against which John the Baptist had issued his warning, "The axe is laid at the root of the tree." And when he added, "Think not within yourselves. We have Abraham to our Father," it is no mere coincidence that those of whom we are thinking, say within themselves, "We have the Church for our Mother." The same spirit of complacent exclusiveness rests on a like insecure foundation. For God is able to do without the Church even as He was able to do without the children of Abraham.

This situation is the more to be regretted inasmuch

as among the Christian Churches outside the Roman there has been seen in the last half-century a progressive recognition of the spiritual unity which underlies all differences of teaching and practice. The age of Protestant scholasticism has passed. Men see that there are more ways than one of coming to Christ (John i. 36, 41, 43), more ways than one of interpreting Him. Some of the rigid formulations of the Reformers (following Augustine and others of the Fathers) have given way before the experience of fellowship with Him and peace with God due to simple faith in Christ. Men who have this experience come together from many different Churches or "denominations," and realise that profound unity for which Jesus prayed—in the sense in which He prayed for it; "that they all may be one, as thou, Father, art in me, and I in thee," words which have nothing to do with institutional unity. For the unity which Jesus had with the Father was at the moment of His speaking just everything but a visible union. What the Reformed Churches are realising with great thankfulness is this spiritual unity springing from a common relation to Christ. It is this relation to Christ which is our criterion of a Christian. The Catholic criterion of a Christian is a man's relation to the Pope.

There is another matter connected with the Church as an Institution, one to which we should shrink from referring, were it not for the extravagant claims which the Roman Church makes to be the only true Church, that which represents Christ to men, an "extension of the Incarnation." We cannot but raise the problem,

How comes it that in so many Catholic countries the Church has been and is the object of such fierce dislike, amounting to hatred, by the common people? It found classical expression in France, which had been known as "the elder daughter of the Church," when Voltaire cried out, "*Écrasez l'infâme*," meaning, "Away with this horrible clericalism." It broke out in violence and cruelty at the time of the Revolution. In our own time it has manifested itself most tragically both in Spain and in Mexico, each of them a "most Catholic" country. There, when the population gets out of hand, it appears to wreak its fury first on Church buildings, and then on the personnel of the Church. This is all the more extraordinary in view of the vast flood of social services and charities of which the Church has for centuries been the channel. Through hospitals, asylums and schools and the devoted services of thousands of monks and nuns it has ministered unceasingly to the needs of all classes of the people. And it must be assumed that a vast number of these "religious" do conquer the respect and affection of those to whom they minister. But there is something in the Catholic system which neutralises their efforts, and brings upon other representatives of the Church suspicion and dislike.

Among the probable causes we should place first the fact that the hold of the priest upon the rank and file is ultimately due to fear—fear of Purgatory, fear of what the priest can do if he is offended. Such fear is ultimately based upon ignorance, and gives way before the advance of knowledge. Then the first doubt as to the reality of Purgatory or the value of Indulgences brings the reflection that these beliefs are a source of vast revenues for the Church. The arrogance of many ecclesiastics, the lowest as well as the highest, constantly wounding men's self-respect, coupled with the perpetual demands for payment for all kinds of religious services, these things account for the suppressed fury which manifests itself in these outbreaks. We have, indeed, a reproduction of the conditions which went before the Reformation. Luther, as we have seen, did not at first challenge the Catholic system or Catholic doctrine. In his famous Theses he challenged only the gross abuse of Indulgences. But his brave attack upon these proved to be a spark which set light to a vast mass of indignation which was seething below the surface in Germany. Germany found what these modern countries have not yet found, powerful voices to express these pent-up feelings. One of Luther's Theses ran, "Christians should be taught that, if the Pope knew about the oppression brought by the preacher of Indulgences, he would rather see St. Peter's burned to ashes than have it maintained by skin and flesh and bone of their sheep." The heart of the German had already turned away from the Roman Church. He had discovered its true character as an Institution. Ulrich von Hutten, a layman, wrote: "You have made the house of prayer into a den of thieves; you are trafficking in spiritual things, in Christ Himself, in the Holy Ghost. Is it not the duty of men to fight against you more valiantly than against the Turks, and to rid the world of you who traffic in God and His altars and sacraments, in the heavens and all heavenly things?" Luther started the Reformation without intending it. As a revolt against Rome it had begun before he had formulated his evangelical interpretation of Christianity. His task was to guide the Reformation, his difficulty to control it.

The same forces are at work to-day to produce in countries which have been fanatically Catholic the same hatred of the Church as an Institution.

SCRIPTURE AND TRADITION

THE doctrine concerning Scripture to which the Roman Church is pledged is one of extreme fundamentalism. All the books of the Old and New Testament, together with the Apocrypha (including, therefore, such productions as the tale of Tobit and the legend of Bel and the Dragon), are proclaimed to have been dictated by God, and to be, therefore, entirely free from error of any kind. Like so many other doctrines of the Roman Catholic Church, this one is held with the utmost tenacity and promulgated as part of the "Catholic faith," but its practical effect on the thought and life of the Church is negligible. As regards the lay members of the Church we have it on good authority that "Catholics are not interested in the Bible." Some shrink from reading it through a subconscious fear that they might be tempted to use their private judgement and raise questions about the teachings of the Church. Others, making the attempt, find themselves entirely at a loss through want of instruction in the history and use of the Bible. It is no good reply (although it is made) that abundant use is made of Scripture in the services of the Church, for one of the rules which is almost universally observed is that these services shall not be in the language of the people. Thus the intellectual background against which these services are performed is not the Word of God but what the worshippers have learnt as "the Catholic faith." Augustine said very truly that a sacrament is a "picture of the Word," but how if there be no Word understandable by the people of which the Sacrament can serve as a picture? The attitude of the Roman Church to the Scriptures has not been at all consistent at all times and in all places. It has varied from toleration to prohibition and even destruction of the sacred books. No modern Catholic would venture to repeat the judgement of English Catholic Bishops upon Tyndale's translation, "A certain heretical and damnable book called the New Testament." But the general tendency has been sternly to discourage the reading of the Bible by the laity so that the fact that the Church proclaims it to be "inspired" is of no practical importance for them.

Neither is it of any real importance for the cleric or the theologian. He believes the Bible to be infallible, not because he has tested it or weighed the evidence against the statement, but simply because the Church says so. It makes no difference to him that any careful student of Scripture may discover quite a number of minor inaccuracies, unimportant historical mistakes and slight discrepancies; but besides these which do not affect the contents of Divine Revelation he cannot but observe and be perplexed by more serious discrepancies or contradictions. Thus, to take only two examples, did our Lord say, "Blessed are ye poor," as Luke has it (vi. 20), or did He say, "Blessed are the poor in spirit," as Matthew reports (v. 3)? Or, more serious still for practical reasons, did He in forbidding divorce lay down an absolute rule, as Luke gives us to understand

(xvi. 18), or did He make a very important exception, as Matthew testifies (v. 32; xix. 7), a problem which, as Bishop Gore said, can never be solved. Questions such as these the Catholic scholar is prohibited from raising, and, in fact, they do not matter to him, because for him Scripture, however infallible it may be, is not the supreme authority. Or, if his scholarly instinct forbids him simply to ignore such questions he has recourse to disingenuous evasion. This is the case with that great New Testament scholar Lagrange, who knows as well as anyone else that the closing verses of Mark (xvi. 9-20) do not belong to the original Gospel, but must not say so. He escapes the dilemma by pronouncing these verses to be "canonically authentic," leaving his readers to infer that though the Church pronounces them to be authentic they are not really an authentic part of the Gospel. The case is worth noting, for it prepares us to recognise innumerable cases of the same kind in Roman Catholic theologians and historians, cases of "manipulating truth."

Scripture is not for the Catholic the supreme authority because, in the first place, he sets another authority upon the same level and even above it, and that is the authority of Tradition. It would be strange, were it not just one of many similar facts, that the Church so quickly ignored the grave warning against putting "tradition" above revealed truth which Jesus gave to the Pharisees, "Ye leave the commandment of God, and hold fast the tradition of men" (Mark vii. 8). The situation is exactly parallel. It was a saying of a famous Rabbi that "words of Sopherim (or Scribes) are more beloved than words of the Law." The Council of Trent definitely put "tradition" on the same level with Scripture. It declared that the Council "receive and venerate with equal piety the books both of the Old and of the New Testament, and also the tradition concerning faith and morals as if dictated either orally by Christ or by the Holy Spirit and preserved by continual succession in the Catholic Church." But in practice, if it came to an issue between Scripture and tradition, it was Scripture that had to give way. Herein the Church once more served itself heir to Pharisaism with what Montefiore calls "the ominously increasing Oral Law."

Strangely enough, in the course of recent negotiations between the Anglican and the Roumanian Churches the English delegation agreed that "nothing contained in tradition is contrary to Scripture." And the delegation did not really help matters by the very ambiguous definition which it gave of "tradition." "By holy tradition we mean the truths which came down from our Lord and His Apostles, and have been defined by the Holy Councils or are taught by the Fathers, which are confessed unanimously and continuously in the undivided Church." Here are four conditions of accepting a "tradition" as true. If all four are insisted upon, it may be safely said that few indeed are the traditions which can stand the test.

The fact is that the word itself is one of most elastic meaning. It may cover anything from a highly probable historical fact to the vision of a neurotic woman, provided only that it rests not on strictly historical evidence, but, at least in its earliest stage, upon hearsay. A fancy, an idea, a tale, a doctrine, a dogma—these are the stages through which many of the Catholic traditions have demonstrably passed. Somebody thinks it, or somebody does it. Others pick up the idea or follow the example. The idea spreads, the practice extends, till it attracts attention from people of some authority. By them it is either adopted or turned down. If adopted it becomes general, and ultimately, being accepted by Council or Pope, is proclaimed to be part of the Catholic faith. That is the life-history of many things in Catholic faith or practice for which justification is claimed from tradition. Of the great mass of traditions there are only three which can claim to fulfil even approximately the conditions laid down by the aforesaid delegation. One is the adoption of the first day of the week as the Christian day for rest and worship; a second is the transference of the celebration of the Lord's Supper from the evening to the morning; and a third is the admission of women to the Sacrament. Of these changes there is no literary record whatever. But, although they do not fulfil the first condition, inasmuch as, though they are not "truths which came down from our Lord and His Apostles," they were "confessed unanimously and continuously in the undivided Church." At the other extreme stands a very large proportion of the things which a Romanist is required to believe, from the presumptuous claim to know that the Virgin Mary was born free from original sin to the legend of the Casa Santa, which asserts that the home

N*   187

of the Holy Family at Nazareth had been transported by angels from Palestine first to the neighbourhood of Trieste and afterwards to the district of Ancona, where it now stands and attracts great numbers of pilgrims. Someone saw it being carried through the air. His story was believed by increasing numbers of people, and was finally pronounced to be true by a Church Synod in Spain. It is on a tradition no more reliable that one of the most popular modern cults is founded. A certain nun reported that our Lord had appeared to her in a vision, and opening His breast had shown her His burning heart within. Again the story was accepted, caught the popular imagination, and led to the establishment of a new Cult, that of the Sacred Heart of Jesus. In spite of the fact that a rule laid down by one of the early Councils that no adoration should be offered to the human nature of Jesus or to any part of it, this cult has received official recognition, and now enters into the devotional life of enthusiastic worshippers in all parts of the Catholic world. And the final approval of the Church has been expressed by the canonisation of the nun who said that she had had the vision. She is now known as St. Mary Alacoque.

This instance illustrates as well as any other both the origin of many "traditions" and the value which may come to be attached to them. The fact is that so far is it from being true that the Roman Church represents a system of thought and worship which comes down from Apostolic times, it really bristles with novelties. It would appear that there is hardly anything too absurd or too unworthy of a spiritual religion to meet ultimately with acceptance by the Roman hierarchy, provided that it has strong and widespread popular support, and that it does not involve any challenge to the authority of the Church. As many of our anthropologists are now pointing out, "Custom is king," and not only king, but "the begetter of beliefs," and the Roman Church shows great worldly wisdom by incorporating in its system ideas and practices which are begotten by custom and born of tradition, though they are related to Christianity by nothing but the name.

Even "tradition," like Scripture, plays but a secondary part in the Roman Catholic system. The appeal to either of them is an appeal to reason, and that is barred in advance. The position was accurately described by the late Cardinal Bourne when he said that it made no difference though a man believed all the articles of the Catholic faith *unless* he believed them on the authority of the Church. That explains many if not most of the "conversions" to Romanism. A man may, for reasons which are not really religious reasons, be led to accept "the authority of the Church," and then without further argument he accepts, or, as it is put, "believes" everything the Church teaches.

CATHOLICISM AND MORALS

THE interlocking of religion and ethics, of belief and conduct, is one of the things which mark the superiority of Judaism, the supremacy of Christianity, among the religions of the world. In the Greek world religion and morality were two departments. They had no bearing on one another. The Greek gods, so far as they had any character at all, were a-moral or immoral. The Greek philosophers who studied and taught the principles of morality did not think of looking to religion for its confirmation or support. It made an immeasurable difference that Jehovah the God of the Jews had character, and character which was at least partially known, and, moreover, that knowledge of Him involved a demand for corresponding character in His worshippers. "Ye shall be holy, for I am holy." To Christians the same God had revealed in Jesus Christ a deeper knowledge of His character. And along with that went a demand which went yet wider and deeper. Henceforth the pattern of Christian character and the goal of Christian ambition was likeness to the man Jesus.

According to the New Testament the development of this character is secured, and the shaping of it provided for, in the first place by whole-hearted response to that commandment of our Lord which He made central to all ethical achievement. "Thou shalt love"—God with all thy heart, and thy neighbour as thyself. On this twin commandment, as He says, hangs the whole law. And Paul, reproducing though not quoting the Master, declares that "he that loveth his neighbour hath fulfilled the law." This is indeed the one commandment of our Lord which properly deserves the name, as being valid for all men, at all times and in all places. Other sayings of His which take the form of commandments assume that this one has been accepted, and adopted as a working principle. They show how that principle does work out when it comes to be applied in various circumstances and in particular situations. They are like sign-posts to a motorist who knows the road. And a man knows the road when he has responded to the Great Commandment, when He really *cares for* God, and really *cares for* his neighbour, the man who is thrown across his path.

One governing principle, caring for God and caring for one's fellow-men, called into activity in response to the love of God for men ("We love, because he first loved us"—1 John iv. 19); this principle interpreted and applied to specific moral questions and situations, not without guidance from Scripture, from the Holy Spirit, and from the judgement of others who are adequately Christian—such would appear to represent the outline of the ethical system which reflects the mind of Christ. This is worth thinking about. For it calls attention to the deep distinction between the ethical theory with which we are presented in the New Testament and that which prevailed in Judaism. Judaism in the time of Jesus and for several centuries before that found all the main lines of human conduct laid down in the Law of Moses. In this it had a written code, much of it of great antiquity and all of it held to be of divine authority. It was assumed to be the duty of every Israelite to give literal obedience to these laws. But through lapse of time and changing circumstances such literal interpretation in many cases became impossible, or failed to meet new problems which arose. It is inevitable that a written code should partly go out of date, partly prove insufficient. It is equally inevitable that if it is to hold its place, some way must be found of so interpreting it and so applying it as to make it available in new conditions and in reference to new problems of conduct. It was this necessity which called into existence the class of men known as Scribes. Professional students of the written Law, it was their business to find in the Law an answer to any and every question which might arise as to conduct. No doubt many of the answers which they gave were religiously sound and valuable. Many of the Rabbis were men of high character, and their reputation combined with their learning gave them, in the opinion of pious Jews, unquestioned authority. But the meticulous analysis of human conduct followed by equally meticulous decisions riveted upon them the yoke of external control. Conscience was left no work to do. And many of their decisions were of such a kind as to call down the stern criticism of Jesus (Mark vii. 6 ff.), while others passed the limits of absurdity, such as a decision (based on Scripture) as to which hand a man should use in blowing his nose.

This history finds a remarkable parallel in the Roman

Church. To begin with, Jesus being looked on as a new Moses, it was assumed that His words and the Old Testament provided a written code of eternal validity. For the same reasons as before this code called for authoritative interpretation and application to questions of morality to which it did not directly refer. And this eventually became the work of a professional type among the Roman clergy, known as "moral theologians." They have followed faithfully in the steps of the Jewish Scribes or Rabbis, and have produced many large works dealing minutely with every conceivable form of human wickedness and moral degeneracy. It is part of a priest's education to study these books, though much of the contents is horrible, and part of his duty to use them in probing the conscience of a penitent in the confessional. There is hardly anything which a man can do or can leave undone which is not covered by some section or clause in this written code, the "moral theology" used in the Roman Church. Whatever moral benefit a man may receive from instruction of this kind, it is clear that the method begins with his complete submission to the priest, an abdication of the freedom unto which "Christ hath made us free." The Church has outdone even the Scribes in riveting a yoke of bondage on its members (Gal. v. 1). It has imposed on them not only a code of moral law but also an authoritative interpretation of it which gives to one man tyrannical power over his fellow-man. Paul had only too good reason to say, "The written code killeth"; he could say with equally good reason, "The Spirit maketh alive" (2 Cor. iii. 6).

It is obviously not possible to describe here, still less to examine, the vast mass of instructions and precepts which make up this moral law of the Roman Church. Neither would it be of much avail, seeing that though this law is authoritative for the Church, the individual priest himself is also an authority, guided no doubt, but not controlled by, the written code; and no one knows exactly how any particular case may be, or has been, handled by any particular priest. It is worth while, however, to try to recognise what is the Catholic mentality which lies behind this complicated system, and may also be presumed to provide the motive which guides a priest in the use he makes of it.

"Blind" was the most penetrating description which our Lord gave of the Pharisees. Blind to moral issues and to the moral principles which were bound up with their religion. Blinded by their devotion to an external institution, the Law, and by their punctilious perform-ance of its requirements, blinded by their own religious-ness so as not to see what God doth require of men, justice and mercy and truthfulness. Catholicism as an institution is open to the same charge as Jesus levelled against Pharisaism (Matt. xxiii. 23). It omits "the weightier matters of the law." The history of the Catholic Church displays a mentality which con-sistently subordinates justice to policy, mercy to hatred and truthfulness to the interest or supposed interest of the Church. Saint Bernard has not a few claims to sainthood, and yet an ecclesiastic who knew him well wrote to him: "You perform all the diffi-cult religious duties: you fast; you watch; you suffer;

but you will not endure the easy ones; you do not love."

Again and again has the Catholic Church turned a deaf ear to the cry for Justice. No more striking illustration could be asked for than the case of which we ourselves have been witnesses. In the autumn of 1935 a cry for justice went up from a nation in Africa, one which had been formally admitted to a common status with others in the League of Nations, one which at least named the name of Christ. It cried out for justice first against unprovoked aggression hurled at it by what claims to be a civilised and a Catholic nation. And this cry for justice found no echo in the whole Catholic Church. The Pope, the representative and spokesman of Christ upon earth, as is continually being asserted, uttered what can only be called a bleat conveying no condemnation of the attack but only a plea that the Abyssinians should be treated as kindly as possible. The Roman Church reserves its thunders for heretics, for such Christians as do not accept its views or submit to its authority.

If we enquire after the reason for this complacency, apart from general reasons connected with nationalism and worldly prudence, a special reason may be found in the Concordat which was concluded between the Fascist State and the Catholic Church in 1929. We know the great concessions which were then granted by the State to the Church: absolute sovereignty for the Pope over the Vatican City, giving him the right to call himself a King and to its inhabitants exemption from State taxes and tariffs; formal recognition of the

Roman Church as the State Church of Italy, to the exclusion of any other; a very large measure of control over education. These, together with a large sum of money, represent the price paid by Italy. We do not know what was the price paid by the Church, but if it was an undertaking that the Catholic clergy from the Pope downwards would refrain from all criticism of the policy or actions of the Fascist State, it would not be a bad bargain for Mussolini, and it would go far to account for this shameful indifference to the cry for justice.

But—we need forcibly to remind ourselves—it is the Church of Jesus Christ of which we are writing.

The word "mercy" stands for the most beautiful word in Hebrew, as it does for one of the finest characteristics of human nature. It covers "considerateness," "pity," "mercy," "love." It describes the attitude of God in Christ towards the ignorant and the sinful. But it is no part of the mentality which characterises the Catholic Church as a whole. It is no pleasure to collect the evidence. But we owe it to those who shall come after us that it shall not be forgotten. There were the Albigenses in Southern France, against whom the Pope organised a campaign. After heroic resistance in the mountainous district of the Cévennes they were practically exterminated. In 1209 the Papal legate reported on the capture of Béziers, their principal town, "our men sparing neither rank, age nor sex, slew about twenty thousand men with the edge of the sword; and when a huge slaughter of men had been made, the whole city was pillaged and burnt, the Divine vengeance

wondrously raging against it." The Archbishop of
Toulouse was said to have destroyed half a million of
lives. The Pope wrote letters praising God for the
success of the campaign. The Oecumenical Council of
1215 called upon secular rulers to exterminate all
heretics. A similar fate befell the Waldenses, whose
blood John Milton in a famous sonnet called upon God
to avenge. These were in no true sense heretics. They
were evangelical Christians, declining allegiance to
Rome. Later on came St. Bartholomew's Day with its
slaughter of twenty-five thousand Huguenots in Paris,
and followed by similar massacres all over France. It is
not too much to say that France has suffered permanent
moral impoverishment through the destruction and
expulsion of the Huguenots. Once and again, at times
of great national crisis, the nation has marked the nature
of this loss by calling Protestants to positions of great
responsibility.

Persecution of "heretics" to the death began about
A.D. 1200 and continued for some six or seven centuries.
And for nearly as long there was not only the general
massacre occurring from time to time, but the continuous work of the Inquisition, which was specially
active in Spain and France. There is no darker blot
on human history than the record of the Inquisition.
It was not only the actual cruelties which it inflicted
upon men and women alike, but the terror which it
created in the minds of masses of people who had not
actually fallen into its hands. There was the devastating
fear of the informant who might anonymously communicate to the priest some hasty speech, the dread of

secret arrest, secret trial, tortures of fiendish ingenuity and then the stake. The motive for such practices was not merely cruelty, but a desire to terrorise the people in general, with a view to keeping them submissive to the Church.

These things are recorded with great fullness and with full documentary evidence in H. C. Lea's *History of the Inquisition*. And the awful story is summed up by W. H. Lecky, an impartial historian, thus: "Almost all Europe, for many centuries, was inundated with blood, which was shed at the direct instigation or with the full approval of the ecclesiastical authorities. That the Church of Rome has shed more innocent blood than any other institution which has ever existed among mankind will be questioned by no Protestant who has a competent knowledge of history."

It is sometimes urged on the other side that "the Protestants were as bad." If this means that there was a time when many Protestants still believed that it was right for the Church to suppress false teaching by force, and even to call on the State to execute the heretic, the saying is true. But its force is turned by two considerations. The first is that the Protestants had not un-learnt all the false doctrines with which they had been familiar in Catholicism. The whole of the new truth which had been shut up in the Gospel was not at once made plain to them. Some of it, indeed, remained undiscovered for three centuries or more. The fact that slavery is in utter contradiction to the will of God is an exact parallel. But Protestants discovered the duty of toleration long before they discovered the iniquity of slave-holding.[1] The second consideration is that, whereas Protestants long ago repented and do still repent of such persecution as must be laid to the charge of their forefathers, no Catholic authority, corporate or individual, has ever expressed repentance or remorse for the Church's part in instigating massacres and maintaining the Inquisition.

If, however, the saying that "the Protestants were as bad" is taken to mean that either in extent or in absence of justification upon non-religious grounds the "persecutions" for which they bear the blame were at all comparable to those for which the Roman Catholic Church was responsible, the statement is simply not true. As regards the extent of persecution to death, England and Scotland are probably the only two countries in which Protestant authorities went that length. And in face of the groundless statements which are made by Romanist apologists it may be well to put down the facts. The *Catholic* estimate for the whole number of Catholics martyred in England between 1535 and 1681 (nearly 150 years) amounts to 253—fewer, that is to say, than the number of heretics burnt in Mary's reign of three years (277) and about as many as were sent to the stake by Torquemada in two years (*Cadoux*). Moreover, the fact that the majority of the Catholics who were executed in England were condemned for "treason," not for "heresy," is not to be dismissed as a Protestant excuse. The Roman Church

[1] Professor Kantorowicz, in his penetrating analysis of the British character, traces the spirit of tolerance which he admires in our race to the influence of Calvinism.—*Spirit of British Policy* (p. 133).

chose not only to be a political power but frequently to interfere in the political affairs of other countries. Its agents were very often priests. The Pope had "deposed the English sovereign." Was it not the duty of Roman priests in England to intrigue against her? In the troublous times of the Stuarts and the Commonwealth, when the Church was certainly intriguing in English politics, it would be small wonder if a large number of these "martyrs" were rightly condemned for political treason.

It is right to say that in quite recent times voices have been heard from official as well as unofficial quarters in the Roman Church deprecating any intention on the Church's part to challenge toleration when it has once been established in a State. But the change, when there is a change of opinion, is wholly due to expediency, and does not involve any change of principle. Voices speaking with not less authority still proclaim their agreement with Thomas Aquinas that heretics, whom he defines as "those who profess the Christian faith, but corrupt its dogmas," must be handed over to the secular arm for capital punishment. The Church recognises baptism as valid, even when not performed by a Roman priest, and on that ground claims jurisdiction over all baptized Protestants. And that jurisdiction does not in theory stop short of power to order the State to send them to the stake.

A third of the qualities which essentially belong to the mentality of a Christian is what New Testament writers call "faith," in one of several meanings which belong to the word (Gal. v. 22, etc.). It stands for Good Faith,

Truthfulness, Honour between man and man. In saying that this does not enter into Catholic mentality we do not for a moment suggest that in matters of everyday life a Catholic is not as scrupulous as other Christians in telling the truth. But it is to be feared that in certain circumstances he is not without encouragement from his Church to use language which is intended to deceive. That he is under no obligation to tell the truth to a "heretic" in itself subordinates the sacredness of truth to the interests of the Church. It was Innocent III who said, "Faith is not to be kept with him who does not keep faith with God"; and, of course, it lay with the Church to decide who fulfilled that condition. John Huss went to the Council of Constance under a safe-conduct from the Emperor Sigismund himself, "to go, stay and return." When he got to Constance he was at once imprisoned, tried and burnt, despite his appeal to Sigismund in person. And even within his own Church the Catholic may be instructed how to use the art of Mental Reservation. An authorised book on Moral Theology suggests how a woman accused of infidelity may give half a dozen answers which sound true but are really false. A Catholic who is asked by a Protestant whether he belongs to the Reformed Church is authorised to reply "Yes," and is encouraged to think that it is not a lie, because the Catholic Church was "reformed" by the Council of Trent, and there are, moreover, chapters in its proceedings which are headed *de reformatione*.

The casuistry contained in these books is by no means exclusively directed to discovering or displaying the guilt of an offender. Its purpose is often to point out a back door by which he can escape from acknowledging his guilt. It is to this extent modelled on the casuistry of the Pharisees, illustrated in Matthew xxiii. 16. If a man came to them concerned about an oath which he had sworn by the Temple or the Altar, they said to him, "That does not matter, if thou hast not sworn by the gold of the Temple." The confessional might thus become a means of education in the evasion of truth. That this was characteristic of the Catholic morality in the fourteenth century we learn from the caustic comment on pilgrims who had returned from Rome which we find in *Piers Plowman*: "They had leave to tell lies all their lifetime after."

And when it comes to controversy on dogma or history it does appear from innumerable cases that a Catholic considers himself free from allegiance to truth. The early history of the Church provides famous and startling illustrations of this in the Forged Decretals and other documents which were put forward in support of the Papal claims. They did their work in an uncritical age, and are now admitted to be forgeries even by the Catholics themselves. But the Church continues to enjoy the prestige and the authority which were built upon these false foundations. Thus the claim to sovereignty over part of Italy was made to rest upon a fable about Constantine invented in the fifth century to the effect that having been healed of leprosy by the Pope Sylvester, the Emperor bestowed the sovereignty over Rome itself and much adjacent territory upon the Pope and his successors. And the strange thing is that this wild story is still read by the Roman priest in his Breviary.

It would be tedious and unprofitable to collect illustrations of ecclesiastical duplicity and indifference to truth such as are scattered over Catholic history and Catholic controversy. We shall content ourselves with evidence from Catholic sources, and chiefly from the Life of a great Catholic ecclesiastic, itself the work of a Catholic pen. One of the most influential writers on Moral Theology whom the Roman Church has ever had was Alfonso Liguori. He was canonised in 1839, proclaimed a Doctor of the Church in 1871, and his works, solemnly pronounced to be free from error, still exercise great influence on all questions of morals. Yet a really great Catholic scholar, Döllinger, has pronounced these works to be "a storehouse of error and lies."

The Life of Cardinal Manning by Purcell is surely the most devastating biography which was ever written by one who professed to be an admirer. Was there ever intrigue more daringly conceived or more ruthlessly pursued than that by which Manning secured the exclusion of Errington from the Archbishopric of Westminster, to which he had been solemnly appointed "colleague and successor," and to which he should have succeeded when the See became vacant. The Pope himself expressed his cynical amazement at Manning's success when signing the final decree, "It is a *coup d'état* of Almighty God." Was there ever anything more disgraceful of its kind than the trick by which Manning tried to prevent Newman becoming a Cardinal (*Life*,

o*

ii, 560). The statement which appeared in *The Times* that Newman had "refused the purple" undoubtedly came from Manning, and was undoubtedly untrue. "It could only come," Newman wrote to the Duke of Norfolk, "from one who not only read my letter, but, instead of leaving the Pope to interpret it, took upon himself to put an interpretation upon it, and published that interpretation to the world." And it was Manning himself who was carrying that letter to the Pope! On another occasion, Newman wrote to Manning, "I can only repeat what I said when you last heard from me, I do not know whether I am on my head or my heels when I have active relations with you."

And there is evidence of the same mentality in Newman himself. There can be no doubt that in the case of Newman *versus* Kingsley the jury of public opinion, in giving its verdict as it did in favour of Newman, was misled by a subtle intellect and a wonderful style pitted against a passionate love of truth and rough and ready reasoning. We cannot but accept the verdict of Lord Acton, whose name stands so high with us all: "Newman is never the servant, he is always the manipulator, of truth."

These things are not intended to blacken the character of either of these ecclesiastics, but to illustrate the fact that there is in the Catholic mentality an indifference to truth at least in matters bearing on religion or the Church. Manning was not a hypocrite in the popular sense of the word. He was not a bad man pretending to be good. His private papers and letters are sufficient evidence to the contrary. But it

would be difficult to acquit him of hypocrisy in the
sense in which our Lord uses the word. The really
characteristic thing about the Pharisees whom He
charged with hypocrisy was their blindness, blindness
to moral issues and moral obligations. And this blindness was directly due to their exaggerated devotion to
the externals of religion, to the Law as a sacred institution and to the punctilious discharge of its requirements.
It would be difficult to deny that Manning was similarly
blind, and for the same reason—an exaggerated devotion
to the Church as an Institution, and an Institution of
the particular type which was demanded by a party in
the Church, the Ultramontanes, to which he belonged.
Intoxicated by his own ambition, he identified his
personal will with the will of God and dismissed all
scruples in order to bring it about. It is part of our
case against Romanism that in the supposed interests
of the Church it tolerates and encourages this indifference to a fundamental principle of Christian morality.
As Lord Acton, himself a Catholic, put it in writing to
Gladstone, "Ultramontanism promotes untruthfulness,
mendacity and deceitfulness."

The Nemesis which follows on all this is terrible.
It has been pithily expressed thus: "There is some
way the soul works so that you can't see truth if you
give up telling it."

We cannot pass over the attitude of the Roman
Church to morality in the narrower sense of the word
when it refers to the relations between the sexes. It
has through the confessional power and opportunity to
guide and control these relations in a way that no other

Church can do, or, indeed, desires to do. Before discussing its methods we may consider for a moment the results. It is very commonly asserted that one result of the Catholic system is seen in a comparison of the statistics of illegitimacy in Catholic and in Protestant countries respectively. This is said to be much more prevalent in the countries which are Protestant. The statement must, however, be dismissed as untrue. According to the figures given in the *Statesman's Yearbook* for 1917, the proportions of illegitimate births were then 85 per 1000 in Roman Catholic states against 74 per 1000 in Protestant (*Coulton*). But the control of the priest extends to the married state itself. How it is used by individual priests by way of question or suggestion we, of course, cannot tell. But we must refer again to the handbooks on Moral Theology which are put into his hands, partly to guide him in the Confessional. There is still in use by Roman priests to-day a book by a Jesuit Father in the eighteenth century, which is of such a character that it drew damning criticism from one who was himself a Roman prelate. "Moral Theology is of such a kind that pure-minded young people should be on their guard against coming in contact with it, lest they fall into shameful misdeeds. What filth is not found in these handbooks. I confess that I have learnt from Sanchez more abominations than I could have learnt from the most abandoned people. Ovid and Horace compared with Sanchez are reading for a nunnery." And then he mentions half a dozen other writers of similar books, and describes them as procurers to the lords of hell.

Heiler, who gives this quotation, himself says, "One is tempted to reckon many features of these books to the literature of pornography. They ought not to bear the *Imprimatur* of the Church, but to take the first place in the *Index* of prohibited books. Yet they are approved by the Church, studied by priests, and may supply questions in the confessional."

That the Roman Church has been a factory of this sort of literature is the ultimate result of its having long ago committed itself to a system of legalistic morality. Just as the Pharisees sought to secure a righteousness of their own by punctilious observance of a legal code of morals, and their successors the Rabbis sought to enforce the application of the code to every conceivable circumstance of human life, so the Catholic Church has felt itself called on to analyse every conceivable form of human frailty and wickedness, in order that the priests may have a written rule to act upon.

With what relief do we turn from all this and the degradation to which it leads to the standard of the New Testament. "Fornication and all uncleanness or ungoverned self-indulgence, let it not be once named among you, as becometh God's people." "It is a shame even to speak of those things which are done of them in secret" (Eph. v. 3, 12).

As to the married state itself the Roman Church of to-day prides itself upon its stern prohibition of divorce, claiming to give literal obedience in this matter to the command of Jesus. But this has not been always its attitude. There was a time in the history of the Church when divorce was permitted just as there was a time

207

when a marriage was admitted to be valid though the ceremony did not go beyond a mutual acceptance of each other as man and wife. And, as we have seen, the present prohibition of divorce is qualified in practice by the possibility of getting a marriage "annulled" on the ground that the parties are related within prohibited degrees. At the same time the Church absolutely refuses to recognise as valid any marriage which has not been celebrated by a Roman priest. And the Concordat between the Italian State and the Papacy, which has already been referred to, has led to a defiance of the universal Christian standard which is hardly credible. It is now possible for a man in Italy to have two wives living at the same time, one of them recognised by the State and the other by the Church.

This is a matter which throws such a startling light upon Catholic mentality in relation to morals that the facts should be stated in some detail. They will be found in consecutive numbers of the *Hibbert Journal* for 1936. But it will be sufficient to examine the article in the July number. It is written by Father Dempsey, S.J., and purports to be a reply to the very serious charge which was made in the January number. But the careful reader will not fail to perceive that the writer does not deny the charge, that, indeed, he rather glories in this new assertion of the Church's dictatorial powers. He admits that among the Instructions recently issued by the Vatican to the parish priests in Italy is one to the effect that if a previous civil marriage (a marriage before a Registrar and not in church) is an impediment to one of the parties being married by a priest to another person, the priest is not to decide the matter himself but refer it to the Bishop. If he judges it well, the religious marriage can then take place. The priest is reminded that it is no use for him to register such a marriage with the civil authorities. Obviously not, for all the civil rights of a wife already belong to the first wife; in the eye of the law the second "wife" has no rights at all. To Father Dempsey this appears nothing more than the logical outcome of the Church's assertion that a civil marriage is no marriage at all, the parties to it are "living in sin." That one of these parties should be so living seems to be no barrier to his being admitted to the "sacrament" of marriage with another woman.

But, apart from all the minor consequences and implications of this amazing arrangement, there is the astounding fact that it gives the sanction of a Christian Church to bigamy. Let us be clear about this. It means that, according to Instructions issued from the Vatican to parish priests, a Catholic in Italy may have two wives, one recognised by the State but repudiated by the Church, and one ignored by the State but recognised by the Church. We have seen already how the mentality of the Catholic Church in relation to morals "passes over" the fundamental Christian principles of justice and mercy and honour (Matt. xxiii. 23), denying them in the interest, or to further the worldly ambitions, of the Church. Thus to grave departure from the Gospel in teaching, in worship and in essential character we have to add quite as grave departure from the revealed standard of Christian morals.

209

THE AUTHORITY OF THE CHURCH

AGAIN and again in the foregoing pages we have found that for the Catholic, whether priest or layman, the final arbiter in all matters of uncertainty or dispute is the Church. The Church dictates the use to be made alike of Scripture and of tradition; it sets aside the evidence of history, prohibits the use of reason in matters connected with religion, and silences the voice of conscience. It roundly and categorically denies the right of the individual to form or hold any opinion of his own on these matters which concern his relation to God and his eternal welfare. And all this it does on the ground that from the beginning the Church has been endowed by Christ with an authority which is not less than Divine.

We remind ourselves that by "Church" is meant in this connection not the whole Body of Christ, not even such part of it as belongs to the Roman obedience, but the clergy in all its grades from Pope to parish priest, and more particularly the ruling class within the clergy. This authority bestowed by Christ is understood to reside in each descending grade, to be exercised within the jurisdiction committed to it. Thus every parish priest is in relation to his flock a little Pope, sharing in the "authority of the Church," limited in its exercise only by the ascending series of officials who are above him. The Papacy is in fact a "totalitarian State," such

as we see now in Germany and in Italy, where the common people find themselves under a local Dictator as well as under a supreme Dictator, who lives in the capital.

The claim to this supreme authority over the thoughts and lives of men is made, therefore, not only on behalf of a single infallible Pope, but also on behalf of a vast number of individual men, each within his own sphere. It is therefore of the first importance to ascertain and examine the grounds on which this claim is made. For vast numbers of ordinary Catholics in various parts of the world the only ground for the claim they feel is that fear of hell which Robert Burns called "the hangman's whup." And the Roman Church is to-day paying the penalty for having through all these centuries relied so largely upon this fear. For when this fear of an eternal hell with its material flames gives way before education and common sense, not only is there nothing left to take its place, but there follows a fierce reaction on the part of great sections of the population who recognise that they and their forefathers have been the victims of organised deceit and exploitation.

With educated men and women, of course, the situation is different. They require to be intellectually persuaded that this claim for complete submission to the Roman Church is well and truly grounded in fact, in history and in the Christian revelation. And here, though here only, the Catholic Church makes an appeal to reason. It is indeed compelled to. Facing an educated human being who doubts or disputes its authority, it must begin by producing reasons why he should admit it. And it is his reason which decides. We have, therefore, this paradoxical position that every such person is invited to use his reason to decide that his reason must abdicate; from henceforth he is to be, in matters of religion, as one who has no reasoning faculty.

What then is the case which the Roman Church sets before a man when it invites him to take this extraordinary step? It rests primarily upon our Lord's words to St. Peter as reported in Matthew xvi. 18, 19. When the Apostle had confessed (that is, acknowledged) Jesus to be "the Messiah, the Son of the living God," our Lord in His reply said, "Thou art Peter, and on this rock I will build my church; and the gates of hell (Hades or Death) shall not prevail against it. I will give to thee the keys of the Kingdom of Heaven: and whatsoever thou dost bind on earth shall be bound in Heaven, and whatsoever thou shalt loose on earth shall be loosed in Heaven." On these words (partially supported and interpreted by Matthew xviii. 18 and John xx. 22, 23; xxi. 15-17) the Roman Church bases its threefold claim that to Peter was given the first place among the Apostles, and indeed authority over them; that to him was given the power to forgive sin or to "retain" it; and so to open or close the Kingdom of Heaven to other men; and that to him was given also the power to transmit these powers to such men as he pleased who would come after him. It is this last claim which underlies what has since come to be known as Apostolic Succession. Whatever powers were thus bestowed upon Peter are thus understood to have been passed on to the Bishops of the Church (although these were never known as Apostles) and through them to "priests" whom they ordained. The clear assertion of this claim is found in the Prayer Book of the Church of England, where the Bishop says to the man he is ordaining to the priesthood, "Whose sins thou dost forgive, they are forgiven; and whose sins thou dost retain, they are retained."

The primacy of Peter, his first place among the Apostles, afterwards interpreted as the Supremacy of Peter; the power to forgive sin; the transmission of the first to Peter's successors as Bishops of Rome, and of the second through Bishops to all whom they ordained to be priests; these are the fateful deductions from the words of our Lord on which the Church of Rome bases its claim to infallibility for its Pope and authority over the thinking and the conscience of men.

The interpretation of this passage as conferring on Peter and his successors as Bishops of Rome the supremacy over all other Bishops and unique authority in the Church does not make its appearance before the third century. There was an intermediate stage during which Matthew xvi. 19 would appear to have been taken along with xviii. 18, and the power conferred upon Peter in the first passage recognised as power conferred also upon the group of which Peter was one, whether this group consisted of the Twelve or was still larger. In any case, it was in the first place for the Church as a whole and specially for its constituted authorities, the Bishops, that the claim was made. And, as we have seen, the great struggle within the Church, which lasted for many centuries, was the struggle of the Bishops of Rome to assert their supremacy over all other Bishops, and to concentrate in their individual hands the authority which, as previously understood, Christ had conferred upon the Church. The issue was finally decided in 1870, and what we are concerned with to-day is a Church which has abdicated its corporate authority and placed itself under a single Dictator.

Coming now to our Lord's words as reported in Matthew xvi. 18, 19, the first question is whether they were actually spoken by Jesus. It is the opinion of an increasing number of scholars that they were not so spoken by Him. There are several considerations which point to this conclusion. (1) These words are reported by Matthew alone, the latest among the Evangelists. A glance at the parallel passages in Mark (viii. 29) and Luke (ix. 20) will show first how closely Matthew in xvi. 13-23 is following Mark, as Luke also does, and secondly, how intrusively these verses 17-18 break in. The corresponding passage in Matthew xviii. 18 has also no parallel in either Mark or Luke. Both passages therefore belong to the latest stratum of the Gospel material. (2) There is the inherent improbability that such words would be addressed to Peter. The portrait of him which we can construct from the Gospels is that of a man warm-hearted, impulsive, but unstable. And that is confirmed by at least one glimpse which we catch of him in the Epistle to the Galatians, where Paul describes how he had to withstand Peter at Antioch on account of his "vacillation." A generous impulse had led him on his arrival at Antioch to associate with Gentile Christians, probably at the Lord's Supper. But when "certain came from James," he yielded to their pressure, and withdrew from "intercommunion." In spite of his fine qualities, it is indeed difficult to understand how this man could possibly be likened to a rock. And it calls for a good deal of courage in Roman apologists to ignore the significance of the passage which immediately follows this one. "Peter took him, and began to rebuke him." And Jesus "turned and said unto Peter, 'Get thee behind me, Satan: for thou art an offence unto me: for thine ideas are not those of God, but those of men.'" Again, it is difficult indeed to believe that the man who deserved to be thus addressed should have just before been selected for primacy among his brethren and for the foundation-stone of the Church. It is already obvious that there are formidable difficulties in the way of the Roman interpretation of these verses.

Many are the explanations which have been offered. One lays stress on the fact that in Tatian's *Diatessaron*, which contains the oldest known text of the Gospels, the crucial words are different and in a different order. There we find, "the gates of Hades shall not overcome thee. Thou art Peter." This would confirm the explanation which has been widely accepted, namely, that when Jesus said, "upon this rock I will build my Church," He meant by "rock" either the acknowledgment of Himself as the Messiah which Peter had just made, or (possibly touching His breast) Himself. This last suggestion is supported by Paul's words in 1 Corinthians iii. 11, "other foundation can no man lay than that is laid, which is Jesus Christ." It is also in harmony with the metaphorical use of the word "rock" which is frequent in the Psalms, *e.g.* "I will say unto God my Rock"; "my God and the Rock of my salvation." Moreover, we have the testimony of Cyprian that Christ was known as "the Rock" or "the Stone," which may indicate that down to his time this was the interpretation given to "upon this rock." It was upon His own Person that Jesus would build His Church.

Others again would reject both verses as not authentic words of Jesus, but an interpolation reflecting views which came to prevail towards the end of the first century. Apart from the difficulties already pointed out they lay stress on the strangeness of the style, the use of the word *ecclesia* which is found only twice in the Gospels and both times in Matthew, the combination of such divergent metaphors, the rock and building, the keys of the Kingdom, and the binding and loosing. The verdict of some of these scholars is expressed thus: "This fateful but certainly apocryphal passage" (*Inge*); "It is difficult not to be drawn to the conclusion that the whole passage is the work of the Evangelist" (*Allen*); "In the form in which the words to Peter lie before us they cannot have been spoken by Jesus" (*Weiss*).

But these, of course, are the arguments and the conclusions put forward and adopted by Protestants. And quite naturally (though mistakenly) they are dismissed with little respect by Romanists. They point out that it is too useful for the Protestant case to dismiss the passage as unauthentic or to explain the rock as a metaphor for Christ Himself. Arguments and con-

216

clusions alike are too plainly prompted by Protestant prejudice.

So it is argued, and we shall be content here to register these opinions and the kind of argument by which they are supported; we shall not make any appeal to them but confine ourselves to two further considerations. The first is the nature of the commission to Peter. Does it include a universal jurisdiction over the religious ideas and the conduct of men? In the passage before in Matthew xvi. 19 it bestows on Peter "the keys of the Kingdom" and the power to "loose" and to "bind." It is Catholic teaching that the second clause interprets the first. And the meaning of the second clause is fixed by the use in Rabbinic literature of the words "loose" and "bind." "Binding and loosing means for the Rabbis the allowing or disallowing of particular types of action. The practical effect of the words is to constitute the Apostles a Christian School of Rabbis" (*Streeter*). This does certainly not include power to forgive sin. "Who can forgive sin but God only?" So ask the scribes in Mark ii. 7. And if the other passage (Matt. xviii. 18) reports Jesus as conferring that power, it is not on any individual that He confers it but on a group of His followers. What is really conferred on the Christian community is the power of discipline over its members, as we find it exercised or to be exercised at Corinth. In 1 Corinthians v. 5 an offender is to have his sin "retained"; he is to be delivered over to the Evil One, whom he has made his god. In 2 Corinthians ii. 5-7 a second offender is to have his sin "forgiven"—by the community.

217

"On this rock I will build my Church." Roman Catholics believe and confidently assert that by the "rock" our Lord meant Peter, and they further assert that this has been the opinion, the only opinion, of the Church from the beginning. And Protestants, unconsciously impressed by what they regard as unanimity of opinion throughout the centuries, shrink from challenging it, partly for fear of meeting the retort that they are taking refuge in a quibble. But herein they are too timid. That is not the only explanation which has had currency in the Church. A Roman Catholic Archbishop, who may be accepted as an impartial witness, has been at pains to analyse the opinions on the subject expressed by the Fathers and other authorities of the early and medieval period, and found that only a quarter of them interpret the "rock" as referring to Peter, another quarter take it to signify Christ Himself, and more than half see an allusion to the confession of Jesus as Messiah which Peter had just made. Augustine himself leaves the question open, but inclines to the view that the "rock" is to be understood as Christ Himself. There is, therefore, good "Catholic" support for the opinion that Jesus (possibly indicating Himself by a gesture) declared that His person was the foundation on which His Church would be built.

We are not, however, greatly concerned to ascertain the exact or the full meaning of our Lord's words to Peter, because of a second consideration as to which there is no manner of doubt. The Roman case stands or falls with the truth or otherwise of the assertion that whatever were the powers conferred on Peter, he was also empowered to transmit them, the primacy to his successor as Bishop of Rome, the other powers to such men as he ordained as Bishops; and further, that the same power of transmission has descended from generation to generation. For this assertion there is nothing that can be called evidence. All that can be done is to trace how it gradually took shape. The earliest reference to succession or handing on of any kind is found in the Pastoral Epistles (2 Tim. ii. 2: "The things that thou hast heard of me among many witnesses, the same commit thou to faithful men, who shall be able to teach others also") and in 1 Clement, who says of the Apostles that they "appointed those who have been mentioned, and afterwards added the prescription that when some of the aforesaid died, other approved men should succeed to their ministry" (xliv. 1). It is clear from the context of these passages that the ministry or office which was thus passed on ("with the consent of the congregation") was one of witness to "the faith once delivered to the saints." The importance of this at a time when there were as yet no recognised written documents is obvious. But of the transmission of any other powers or functions—the power to forgive sin or the power to rule despotically—there is not a trace in the Christian literature of the first century. That authority which is claimed to-day is the latest link in a chain which reaches back through many generations. But it is fruitless to trace it back and back, as of course it can be traced, when we come at last to a point where it had a human origin. It is very significant that Ignatius, in spite of his overwhelming anxiety to establish the

P*   219

authority of the Bishop, "has no thought of succession at all" (*C. H. Turner*). What we are reminded of is the Indian rope-trick, when the bystanders are made to see a rope hanging from the sky, but those who know, know that it has been projected from the earth. In other words, at this crucial point, the point at which a man's reason *must* decide, the Roman Church has no evidence at all to offer which can appeal to the faculty of reason. The bestowal of absolute authority upon Peter cannot be proved. The transmission of it is a fable.

But the fallacy of this claim, its inconsistency with the spirit of the Gospel, can be seen in another way. It was not either the purpose or the method of Jesus to leave men in subjection to any kind of authority external to themselves. As has been finely said, "His last word was not 'I say,' but 'you see.'" His first words were words of an external authority, words of One who spoke as a man to men. But those who responded to Him, who consented to His teaching, became aware of an internal authority, one which increased in clearness and influence. They "saw" that what He said was true. It was in this sense that they said, "He speaks with authority, and not as the scribes," who indeed spoke with authority, but not an authority which produced internal assent. And our Lord definitely threw on men the responsibility of using their reason, "Why do ye not decide for yourselves what is right?" (Luke xii. 51). What Jesus sought was the free allegiance of free men. And Paul grasped the same idea, when in Romans xii. 2 he claimed for the community the power to "ascertain what is the will of

God, the Noble, the Well-pleasing and the Ideal," and when he said, "The written code killeth, but the Spirit maketh alive." The guiding power of the Spirit was specially realised in the assemblies of Christians, when, as Paul said, they "heard Christ" and were "taught in him." The authority which they then felt was the internal authority of the Holy Spirit.

It will not be denied that men cannot do without external authority. But the authority which they are invited to recognise is not coercive but persuasive. Such is the authority of Jesus Himself, of the Word of God contained in Scripture and of the Church or community of believers, whether it reaches him through classical documents of the past or through living voices of the present. No true follower of Christ will hastily decide or act in contradiction of any of these. They provide the material for his decision, but that decision is a decision of conscience educated by persuasive authority.

From authority such as this the coercive authority claimed by the Catholic Church differs entirely. The happy consequences following obedience to the Church and the unhappy consequences entailed by disobedience may vary with different grades of intelligence, but, whatever the form it may take, it brings the pressure of fear or of hope to bear upon the individual. The Church promises or threatens consequences which are eternal, and presents itself as the divinely authorised arbiter of his fate. Whereas Christ would ennoble His followers by trusting them and throwing on them the responsibility for the right use of reason and conscience, the Roman Church denies to them the use of each of these supreme qualities of humanity. External authority was conferred by Jesus upon the Christian community represented by Peter and his comrades (if we may accept Matthew's report as genuine), at least to the extent of deciding what was permissible and what was not, and of disciplining its own members by either "forgiving" or "retaining" their sin. In the third and following centuries this claim shrank in one way, expanded in another. It vastly expanded to include unlimited authority over the religious thinking and the consciences of men. It shrank in respect of the number of persons in whom these powers were understood to reside. What had been the prerogative of the local community or church passed into the hands of officials (Presbyter-bishops and local Bishops), was then concentrated in "monarchical" Bishops or in General Councils, and finally concentrated in the hands of a single individual, the Pope. In place of the educated and responsible self-government which Jesus sought to establish in His followers (guided by the Word of God and the common Christian mind), the joyful obedience of free men to Himself alone, men found themselves confronted by a human despotism exercised by all grades of a clerical caste from the Pope downwards, and resting only on self-assertion and force.

The Authority of the Church as interpreted and applied to-day stands in cynical contradiction to the mind and teaching of Jesus. "Neither be ye called masters, for one is your Master, even Christ." (And the word translated "master" means "one who goes before and leads.")

This concentration of supreme authority in the hands of the Pope received final recognition in the proclamation of Papal Infallibility in 1870. Like so many other features of Romanism it was just the recognition in theory of what had already been long acknowledged in practice. It marked the crowning success of a policy which had been pursued with amazing patience and persistence through many centuries. The Decree was carried through the Vatican Council in the face of opposition which though inconsiderable in numbers was very considerable in weight of scholarship and character. The opposition came mainly from France and Germany. The solid nucleus of support was in Italy, and from those Bishops who, accepting the Italian lead, classed themselves as "Ultramontanes." Strangely enough it was an Englishman, Archbishop Manning, who had formerly been a clergyman of the Church of England, who, as an individual, contributed most to their final success. It was a triumph for him and for the Jesuit Order.

The interpretation which Protestants commonly put upon the Infallibility of the Pope is a mistaken one. The doctrine by no means suggests or implies that the Pope is infallible in all circumstances or on all subjects, that he can never be mistaken. The significant words of the Decree run thus: "The Roman Pontiff, when speaking *ex cathedra*, that is, when performing the office of Pastor and Doctor of all Christians, he defines, in virtue of his apostolic authority, a point of doctrine or morals, obligatory for the entire Church—the Roman Pontiff, thanks to the divine assistance which was promised to him in the Most Blessed Peter, enjoys that infallible authority with which the divine Redeemer endowed His Church, when the question arises of defining doctrine concerning faith or morals." It will be noticed at once that according to the terms of this Decree the Pope is declared to be infallible only in certain circumstances and in reference to certain subjects. As to the subjects the range is fairly clear, but the circumstances are left extremely vague. It is only when speaking *ex cathedra* that the Pope is infallible, and that is explained to mean "when he is performing the office of Pastor and Doctor of all Christians." It would appear, therefore, that in order to ensure his proclamation being accepted as infallible he must himself announce that he is to speak *ex cathedra*.

This dogma of Papal Infallibility is therefore of much less practical importance than is commonly supposed. As a matter of fact, no practical use has been made of it since the Council by which it was defined. It had been used in 1854, when, after a perfunctory consultation of some Bishops, the then Pope, on his own authority, laid down the doctrine of the Immaculate Conception of the Virgin. What is of far more importance for its practical bearing on the life of the Church is the general authority which is ascribed to the Pope, quite apart from his "infallibility." This also was laid down by the Vatican Council. Their meaning is here unmistakable. "The Roman Pontiff has not only the office of inspection and direction, but also full and supreme jurisdiction over the universal Church, not only in things which concern faith and morals, but also in things which concern the discipline and government of the Church in the whole universe."

It appears not a little significant that in both parts of this Decree, which is now fundamental to the constitution of the Roman Church, the Pope is described not in terms which place him in any relation to Christ but as "the Roman Pontiff," the pagan title of a pagan office. It was, moreover, a title which had been proudly borne by Roman Emperors. But it had been definitely abandoned by the Emperor Gratian, who saw in the title a symbol of paganism from which he sought to dissociate his Empire. The title "Roman Pontiff" is not one of which the "representative of Christ" upon earth has any reason to be proud. Its readoption by the Popes as the current designation of themselves marks the fact that the Papacy is a human empire using the religious instincts and needs of men to forge fetters on those whom Christ would fain make free.

"My kingdom is not of this world."

"Ye shall know the truth, and the truth shall make you free."

It is instructive to observe how closely the situation we have been examining corresponds to the danger which St. Paul diagnosed as threatening the Church at Colossae. As he had urged the Corinthians, "Make use of the freedom into which Christ has redeemed you. Do not enslave yourselves to anyone," so he writes to the Colossians, "Let no one take you to task in matters of meat and drink, or of festivals or new moons or sabbaths, mere shadows of things to come, whereas the substance is Christ. Let no one cheat you of your prize insisting on submissiveness and the worship of Angels, taking his stand on visions that he has seen." "Why, as though you were still living the life of the world, do you allow yourselves to be dictated to by those who say, 'Touch not, taste not, handle not' (things which perish in the using), in accordance with merely human regulations and instructions? These things have a sound of prudence though they spring from wilful imposition of worship and submissiveness and mal-treatment of the body. They are not really worth anything, but actually minister to the satisfaction of the lower nature" (Col. ii. 16-18, 20-23). It is all, or nearly all there, the Dictatorship, the submission to other spiritual powers than God, the worship of Angels based on reported visions, submission to human authorities and the imposed asceticism which has no real value, but may actually lead to morbid self-satisfaction.

The principal thing that we can learn from this remarkable parallel is that Romanism represents the result of a certain downward drag in human nature, which always takes the same forms and is perpetually challenged by the Spirit of Christ.

CONCLUSION

IT is a curious but not uninteresting reflection that no one who has submitted to the Catholic Church will read this book. To do so would get a man into trouble with his confessor. For it is throughout an appeal to history and to reason. And any such appeal is for a Romanist ruled out in advance as "heresy and treason." Even the appeal to Scripture (and that includes the teaching of our Lord) is for the Catholic layman an act of insubordination. It is also for him futile. For he understands that even Scripture must be interpreted, and may require to be corrected, by Tradition. And even the combined witness of these two authorities must yield to the "authority of the Church," whether it be the authority of Pope, prelate or priest.

Appealing to history, the history of Christian thought, we have seen how as early as the beginning of the second century the Church had gravely departed from "Christ," giving the word a meaning which St. Paul gives it, the message about Christ. This was not the fault of any man or men. It was due to the fact that while the witness was no longer the voice of those who had seen and heard Jesus, or even of those who had been sharers in the "conquering new-born joy," and in the high tides of the Spirit which carried the Gospel triumphing from Jerusalem to Rome, the Church had no collected and authoritative documents of its own. It depended for public reading and personal guidance upon the Jewish Scriptures. And though these Scriptures held in solution much that was afterwards crystallised in the Gospel, they contained much else which, by our Lord, had been either transcended or ignored. Of these things not a few had gone to the shaping of Judaism in the first century B.C., religion as it was understood and taught by the Pharisees. It was easier for those many Christians who had been Jews to believe in Christ and to rejoice in Him as Saviour than to clear their minds of Jewish ideas (such as salvation by merit) with which they had been familiar from childhood. We have to remember that the situation which confronted the Church towards the end of the first century corresponded pretty closely to that which confronts the Church in some parts of India to-day, what is known as mass-conversion. There must have been times and places at which the number of teachers competent to instruct in the principles of the Gospel was quite inadequate to deal with the number of people who required instruction. And if we imagine what the Church in those parts of India might very well become, if left by force of circumstances to shape its own thinking and its own practices, we might get something not unlike the Catholic Church of the Middle Age. It would be a powerful Church, a popular Church, a Church with a strong tendency to polytheism, and by no means averse to adopting any superstition which had a sufficient number of supporters.

We have been examining the character of the Roman Catholic Church, its teaching on religion and on morals and its worship. We have compared these with the teaching and the worship to which the New Testament bears witness as having the authority of Christ, or as representing the authoritative interpretation of His mind by His immediate followers under the guidance of His Spirit. We have freely admitted that neither the offered guidance of the Spirit nor its result in deeper penetration into divine truth was necessarily suspended at any moment in the history of the Church. But obviously such guidance can only be obtained on certain conditions. It can be enjoyed only by those who are truly united to Christ by faith, those who are wholly disinterested. Neither a worldly minded man nor a worldly minded Church can have it. We recognise that such guidance may, indeed must, lead to development in doctrine. Illustrations of such development which is legitimate may be found on the field of ethics in the recognition of the social equality of women, or in the discovery that slavery is contrary to the will of God, and on the field of doctrine possibly in the abandonment of a rigid doctrine of predestination. But we have insisted that in order to claim the assent of Christians, such developments must be true to the original type, must not involve contradiction of any of its essential characteristics. We found these essential characteristics according to the New Testament to be or to include the following:

Faith as trust in God as He is known to us in Jesus Christ, issuing in a personal relation to Him and leading to an increasing knowledge of Him and His way in the world, and to an ordered account of what has thus come to be known, which we call theology.

This faith as trust, the response of man to God's approach to him in Christ, and especially in "him crucified."

This personal relation to God involving and resting upon the forgiveness of sin and reconciliation to the Father.

The gift of the Holy Spirit, who is, in the experience of the Christian, interchangeable with the Risen and Living Christ (see Romans viii. 9-11), doing in him and for him all that Jesus in the days of His flesh did for His disciples.

The Word of God contained in the Bible interpreted to men by the Spirit and especially when they are met together in fellowship with Christ, as the source of knowledge about God, about Christ, and about human duty.

The Word of God, the Sacraments and the Fellowship of Christians as the means of grace which God in Christ has provided for His people, the Nourishment of the Life which is eternal.

The Lord's Supper as a picture of the Word, given to men to help them to realise the real presence of Christ, "known to them in the breaking of bread," and offering Himself as the Bread of Life.

Through the Church or Fellowship of believers the experience of oneness in Christ, and of the guidance of the Spirit into deeper knowledge and understanding of God; and, further to this, an opportunity of so realising fellowship with Christ that men take up life as He took up the Cross, share with Him in the burden of human sin, and so become "priests unto God."

Love, or caring, for God and for other men as the fulfilling of the law, love which changes duty into impulse, external authority into internal aspiration.

These are the governing principles which define the type of religion revealed in the New Testament, which were sealed by the Death and Resurrection of Jesus Christ.

We have seen how at a very early date the Church slipped down from what was involved in our Lord's declaration that the Publican went down to his house "justified" rather than the Pharisee, a declaration which Paul repeated in his own way, "By grace ye are saved through faith, not of works." This departure from the mind of Christ was in itself sufficient to change the character of the Christian message. It substituted for the filial relation between God and man which Jesus sought to establish that contractual relation which underlies the whole Catholic system.

Against the Catholic doctrine that salvation is earned in part at least by the "works" which a man does, with the corollary that those who are Saints have laid up a surplus stock of "merit" which can be applied by the Church for the benefit of other men, we set the principle laid down by Jesus, "When ye have done all those things which are commanded you, say, We are unprofitable servants; we have done that which was our duty to do." This is true so long as men insist (as the Pharisees did) on remaining on a contractual footing with God. They can never produce a margin beyond what is expected from them.

Against the statement of the Athanasian Creed that "He that willeth to be saved, before all things it is necessary that he hold the Catholic Faith . . . which except he believe faithfully, he cannot be saved," we place the fact that to several people, not one of whom had any knowledge of Christian doctrine, our Lord said, "Thy faith hath saved thee; go in peace."

When we hear the Pope acclaimed as "Pope and King," or as "the King of the Kings of the earth," we marvel that he should for one moment be thought of as the representative of Him who said, "My kingdom is not of this world."

When we find Scripture, the revealed Word of God, definitely subordinated to Tradition, we ask, "Are these men deaf to the reproach which Jesus addressed to the Pharisees as those who 'made the word of God of no effect through your tradition.'"

And when we hear of one whom his confessor has bidden to recite as a penance a dozen Paternosters and many more Ave Marias every day, other words of Jesus leap up in our memories, "Use not vain repetitions as the heathen do." They will not, however, occur to the penitent, for he, poor man, does not know the Gospels.

And it is surely very significant that when a Catholic speaks of "conversion," he means conversion to the Roman Church, not conversion to Christ. There is an illuminating sentence in one of Manning's letters, "Our Lady has given us a good covey of converts, some of them likely to be very useful." Does not the spirit which finds expression here come under the scathing criticism addressed by our Lord to the Pharisees, "Ye compass sea and land to make one proselyte?"

In all these cases, and they do not stand alone, we find the Roman Church denying or ignoring express teaching of our Lord. And it is only to ignorance or indifference to that teaching, and the conception of religion which it enshrined, that we can trace the unmistakable departures from type which we find in Catholic worship and moral ideals. We cannot but see in the Mass a travesty of the Lord's Supper; in the worship of the Madonna a fatal intrusion on the unique Sovereignty of God and on the sufficient Saviourhood of Christ; in the worship of Saints a further infringement on the prerogatives of God and the denial of that direct access to the Father which St. Paul hailed as one of the great privileges of Christians; in Purgatory a man-made myth; and in the claim to power to control through Mass and Absolution men's experience of Purgatory nothing but a groundless assertion of the human will to power.

It is these things which a man is called upon to believe if he would be a Catholic, and, what is not less serious, it is these things which are to play by far the largest part in his worship and in his personal religion. Nevertheless, it is hard indeed to deny that, taken together, these things denote a departure from that type of religion which has its classical expression in the New Testament, a departure so far-reaching and so profound that it cannot be justified as legitimate "development." The question, indeed, forces itself upon us, Is Catholicism as embodied and expressed in the Roman hierarchy, doctrines and worship to be regarded as an inferior form of Christianity or as, alike in theory and in practice, a different religion, to be judged no doubt on its merits, but so untrue to the Christian type that it is misleading to give it that name? As we have seen, its genius is rather the genius of Pharisaic Judaism than that of the New Testament. Its connections with what is specifically Christian are formal and unreal. At the heart and core of its system there are principles at work which are alien and even hostile to the fundamental principles of the Gospel, such as the priesthood; material or "objective" sacrifice; control of men by fear; suspension and, in the interest of the Church, denial of the first principles of Christian morality; the encouragement, at least among the clergy, of arrogance, falsehood and cruelty. It professes allegiance to Jesus Christ, but what it demands of men is allegiance to itself. It actually disparages the belief which it demands by proclaiming that, although a man were to believe all that he ought to believe, it would make no difference "unless he believed it 'on the authority of the Church.'" It makes religion a means to an end, and that end is the increase of its own glory and power.

Viewed from outside, the Roman Church may be immensely impressive, its organisation extraordinarily efficient, its worship magnificent. It will not be denied that to many individuals these things make a tremendous appeal. But the questions which every man who is honest with himself must answer before yielding to the appeal are these. Is it a religious appeal? Has it any vital connection with Jesus of Nazareth?

If the impression has forced itself upon us that this Church exercising an authority which is not less than divine, claiming an allegiance such as men owe to God alone, does in effect, though not in words, proclaim itself to be divine, are we not confronted by one who "as God sitteth in the temple of God, showing himself that he is God"?

This is a question which every man must settle for himself. Only let him remember that the price he would pay for accepting the authority of Rome is nothing less than abdication of those elements in his personality which are most akin to God, the de-throning of his reason (so far as religion and morality are concerned) and the giving to his conscience notice to resign.

BOOKS FOR FURTHER STUDY

————o————

LARGE AND COMPREHENSIVE WORKS

Karl Hase, *Handbook to the Controversy with Rome*.
C. J. Cadoux, *Catholicism and Christianity*.
F. Heiler, *Der Katholizismus*.
H. C. Lea, *History of the Inquisition*.
G. G. Coulton, *Five Centuries*.
A. Sabatier, *Religions of Authority*.

SMALLER AND SPECIAL WORKS

E. B. Pusey, *Eirenicon*.
R. Littledale, *Plain Reasons against joining the Church of Rome*.
Karl Heim, *Spirit and Truth*.
Margaret Deanesley, *The Lollard Bible*.
D. Chadwick, *Social Life in the Days of Piers Plowman*.
B. L. Manning, *The People's Faith in the Time of Wiclif*.
A. J. Mason, *Purgatory*.

J. AND J. GRAY, PRINTERS, EDINBURGH